▣ Contents

▣ Welcoming Beacons

Lighthouses were welcoming beacons to seafaring men in bygone days. During the age of sail, these watchtowers, with their warning lights, warned of danger lurking close at hand. Perched at strategic points, the steadfast presence of Maine lighthouses reassured sailors plying the rocky coast in windjammers. Even after power replaced sail, lighthouses were essential to the safety of those who made their living from the sea.

Many stories are told of the men, women, and children whose daily existence was intertwined with that of the sailors whose lives were often dependent upon these guiding lights. Although the sailors, the lighthouse keepers, and their families were forever strangers, their spirits were interwoven as surely as tides rise and fall.

Eventually, these early light keepers were replaced by members of the United States Coast Guard; then came automation and modern technology, in the form of radar and loran. There was no longer a need for humans to keep the beacons lit.

Gradually, the coast of Maine entered a new era. One by one, the manned lighthouses were decommissioned as they were not needed. One by one, those still standing are being rescued by people who refuse to stand by and watch them disappear from the landscape. Although these celebrated structures are part of another life and time, today they are gradually being restored, revisited, and romanticized.

Lighthouses in the Family

I have lived away from the ocean for a short period only twice in my life, and during those times I felt landlocked. Maybe I was destined to use lighthouse motifs in my creative projects because so many of my family members have made their livelihood from the sea and therefore depended on the local lighthouses to guide them safely out and back. Not surprisingly, many of the lighthouse designs on these pages have a personal meaning for me.

MARSHALL POINT LIGHT

Through the years, Marshall Point Lighthouse in Port Clyde, Maine, has stood guard for the lobstering men of my family. My paternal grandfather, Sherman Benner, was a lobsterman, as were his father and *his* father, back through many generations. My father, Henry Benner, drove a trailer truck for a while, but eventually he too turned to lobstering. Although he constantly battled seasickness, even in calm seas, he pulled traps until he was seventy, when the family convinced him it was not wise to be on the water alone.

My maternal grandfather, "Gus" Snowman, was born in Newagen, Maine. As a youth, he fished for lobsters in the

ROCKLAND BREAKWATER LIGHT

shadow of the lighthouse at the Cuckolds. Eventually he married, raised a family, and built a successful construction business, but after retiring he returned to his first love—lobstering. Since he worked from a small boat (an outboard-powered dory), his outer boundary was defined by the Rockland Breakwater Light, one of the twelve sites featured in these pages.

Our oldest son, Tim, served in the Coast Guard, and many of his days in the service were spent in and around the Boothbay and Kennebec River lighthouses. Middle son Michael is a marine engineer helping to design nuclear submarines—the only family member with experience beneath the waves. While attending Maine Maritime Academy, Mike introduced me to Dice Head Light and the rich history of Castine. Youngest son David moved to New York City and worked on Wall Street but had a love/hate relationship with that life. He now buys and ships lobsters. My husband, who is retired, works for him. David's lobster business is named for Islesboro's Grindle Point Lighthouse.

My uncle Weston Thompson spent his adult life as a member of the United States Lighthouse Service. He served at Portland Head Light, at Southern Island in Tenants Harbor, at the Rockland Breakwater Light, and at the light stations on the Cuckolds and Matinicus Rock. After the Coast Guard took over operation of U.S. lighthouses, Uncle Wes continued to serve under the new regime until his retirement. It strikes me as ironic, though, that someone who had once been the man in charge at two "tough duty" stations spent the end of his career "assisting" younger men with far less experience.

My father-in-law, Eino Aho, spent most of his working years fishing on the Grand Banks. Despite coming from a long line of Finnish farmers, he, unlike my father, was never seasick. Eino, too, appreciated the role lighthouses played in protecting the individuals who made their living from an unpredictable ocean.

I am convinced we are a family with salt water flowing through our veins.

— Pat Aho

THE CUCKOLDS LIGHT

◙ About This Book

This is a lighthouse book. This is a quilting book. My hope is that it will bring pleasure to all creative people who love lighthouses or love to quilt—or both.

I've tried to carry the comfortable, personal tone of my quilting classes into the pages of this book by keeping the directions simple and doing the drawings freehand. I want my fellow quilters to simply enjoy being creative rather than worrying about cutting pattern pieces with millimeter-by-millimeter precision or doing the stitching exactly the way I did it. As you pin your appliqué pieces in place, you'll find yourself tweaking a curve here, scootching a placement there, and this is exactly what you should be doing—giving the quilt square your personal touch.

The twelve Maine lighthouses featured in these pages were chosen for their diversity of design, their history, and/or their locale. Each lighthouse square may be used individually or assembled with others for a wall hanging or quilt. If the choice is a quilt, the overall size of the piece can be altered with the addition of sashing (between squares) and borders (around the outside edges of the quilt). Then the assembled quilt can be embellished with the marine-related quilting patterns I have also provided.

In addition to the dozen lighthouses, you will also find appliqué designs for stars and a pesky crow, as well as patterns for patchwork quilt squares featuring a Fresnel lens, a schooner, and a mariner's compass. There are also several "just plain quilting" designs based on nautical themes. Many of these quilting designs can be used for appliqué as well; just remember to add a ⅛- to ¼-inch seam allowance around the edge as you cut them out.

Rather than give down-to-the-last-stitch directions for just a few finished pieces, I've chosen to provide designs and stitching patterns you can use in many different combinations. Each square can stand alone or be combined with others. The examples shown in the photographs are just that—examples. Match them exactly, if you wish, but I hope you will also feel inspired to use them as the starting point for your own quilt projects, large and small. My intention is to allow you, the quilter, plenty of choices in the way you express your appreciation for these coastal beacons by creating your own work of art for future generations to enjoy.

Do you have a favorite lighthouse that you think would make a beautiful quilt square? I hope that this book will be just the first of several collections of quilt designs featuring lighthouses from around the United States, and I welcome your suggestions about lights to include in future books. You can send letters or e-mails via my publisher:

Pat Aho
c/o Down East Books
PO Box 679
Camden, ME 04843

e-mail: books@downeast.com

◩ Achievable Appliqué

*M*any quilters shudder at the mere mention of the word appliqué. They feel this technique is too time consuming, too tedious, too difficult. Nothing could be further from the truth. Appliqué is not as precise as patchwork. Points need not match perfectly. Seams do not have to be exact. It simply takes practice, patience, and persistence.

The appliqué process layers fabric pieces on a fabric base to create a design. Designs with many parts may seem formidable, but they are not. They just take more time to execute.

Appliqué affords a freedom of expression not allowed with patchwork, giving quilters the ability to create an easily recognizable picture.

How to Appliqué

1. Place pattern on the *right* side of fabric and trace around it. This tracing line will be the seam line. Cut around pattern, leaving a ⅛- to ¼-inch margin beyond the seam line. (This margin is the seam allowance.)

2. Fold the seam allowance toward the wrong side of fabric. Do not fold the seams that will be hidden beneath another appliqué piece, however.

3. Baste the folded piece. Set aside. Prepare each piece to be appliquéd this way.

4. PRESS each piece. To press, place the iron on the fabric, then lift it again without moving it from side to side. *(Do not be tempted to skip the pressing step. An iron is one of a quilter's most important tools!)*

5. Position and pin the prepared pieces to the background. Baste to background.

6. Using a size 10 or size 12 quilting needle, slip-stitch each piece to the background. *(Be sure to use a small needle. A regular size 10 needle will not produce nice, tiny stitches.)*

How to Slip-Stitch

1. Hold the work facing you, drawing the needle toward you as it comes through the cloth. Take a tiny stitch in background material. Next, insert needle into folded edge of appliqué piece, directly above the stitch just taken. Bring needle out though the folded edge about ¼ inch away.

2. Take another tiny stitch in the background fabric, directly beneath the point where your needle came out through the appliqué piece. Continue in this manner. If it seems awkward at first, just remember: practice, patience, and persistence.

A Few Appliqué Tips

1. Fold and finger press the background fabric in half and then into quarters. Use this as a guide for placing the pieces to be appliquéd.

2. Tuck the parts to be covered by adjacent pieces *under* those pieces. For instance, on one of the lighthouse squares, a shrub sits beside a tower. Baste the shrub to the background, but **don't fold** under the part of the seam allowance to be covered by the tower piece. The shrub will appear to be behind the tower.

3. To ensure sharp points, fold the point toward the wrong side of the fabric. Press. Then fold in the sides and proceed to prepare for appliqué.

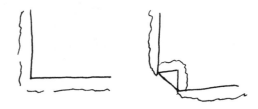

4. Folding and basting take extra time, but the results are well worth the effort. Make sure the folds fall smoothly. Your finished project will show the results!

Fusible Appliqué and Blanket-Stitching

Nowadays we also have the option of using fusible webbing, as described below. If you wish, you can add decorative blanket-stitching around the edges after the pieces have been fused to the background. Blanket-stitch appliqué was popular during the 1920s and 30s. The black stitching still has an informal appeal, and can be added to many of the projects in this book. Today's version can be done either by hand or by machine, and is easy, fuss-free, and fun.

Materials Needed

Background cloth
Cloth for appliqué pieces
Double-sided fusible webbing
Black embroidery floss (if blanket-stitching is
   to be added)

How to Do Fusible Appliqué

1. Cut pieces of fusible webbing and the cloth to be appliquéd. Be sure to cut these pieces slightly larger than the pattern piece.

2. Press webbing to the wrong side of cloth, using a hot, dry iron. Let cool.

3. Now, trace the pattern to be appliquéd onto the paper backing of the fusible webbing. *Note:* When placing a pattern onto the webbing paper for tracing, remember that the pattern needs to be placed right side *down* on the paper.

4. Cut along the tracing line. Repeat this step with each appliqué piece.

5. Arrange each piece, right side up, on the background cloth. When you are satisfied with the placement, peel the paper backing from webbing. Press each piece onto the background cloth.

6. You may choose to leave the appliquéd pieces just as they are, or you may blanket-stitch around each piece. *For hand stitching,* thread a needle with two strands of embroidery floss. Blanket-stitch around each piece, keeping the stitches about ¼ inch apart (see diagram below). *For machine embroidery,* follow instructions for your sewing machine.

BLANKET STITCHING BY HAND

DECORATIVE BLANKET STITCHING ADDS INTEREST TO THE "PESKY CROWS" DESIGN (P. 25).

◙ Projects, Projects, Projects!

*T**he quilt squares and stitching templates in the following pages can be used creatively in a variety of projects: large (bed coverings), small (coasters), and practical (tote bags and pillows). I will start with the flat projects, because many of the procedures used in making wall hangings, quilts, and the like are the same whether you are working with one square or several.*

Flat Projects, Large and Small

Many quilters enjoy the challenge of making a large quilt, while others prefer smaller projects. Either way, the assembly steps are the same.

Today's mattresses and bed coverings are made in several standard sizes, which are listed below for your convenience. However, there is no rule saying that individual quilters cannot alter sizes to fit their own needs.

Bed size	Mattress size	Bedspread size
twin	39" x 78"	79" x 118"
double	54" x 78"	94" x 118"
queen	60" x 78"	100" x 118"
king	72" x 84"	112" x 124"

There are numerous ways to determine which size quilt to make. Following are eight questions you may wish to consider before making a final decision.

1. How will the quilt be used? Will it be used as a bedspread or folded at the foot of the bed? Will it be displayed on a quilt rack or used as a tablecloth?

2. Will the quilt be purely functional, serving as warmth against cold winter nights?

3. Will the quilt squares fit the mattress top exactly? Will you add borders to allow the quilt to hang over the sides of the bed?

4. Will the quilt hang to the floor, or will it be teamed with a dust ruffle and only need to overhang enough to cover the mattress sides? Will borders be added on all four edges, or only to the sides and foot of the quilt?

5. Will there be sashing between the quilt squares, or will the squares butt up against each other with no sashing in between?

6. Will the quilt feature squares of a colorful design alternating with squares of a simple outline-stitched design?

7. If the quilt is to serve as a bedspread, will it cover the pillows or go underneath them?

8. Should the quilt be made with an equal number of squares both vertically and horizontally, resulting in a square format? If the quilt is not going to be used as a bedspread or serve as a table cover, this may be the easiest layout to use.

Preparing Your Fabric

Prewashing fabric is always a good idea, no matter how eager you might be to jump in and start cutting out pattern pieces. The rule of thumb I tell my quilting students is: If there is even a *remote* chance that your quilted project will ever need to be laundered, then be sure to machine wash and dry the original fabrics.

I always buy quality fabrics, but I know many quilters purchase less expensive yardgoods. Sometimes we just have to have a particular color or print. Not prewashing these fabrics can raise havoc later.

Putting Those Squares Together

There is one hard and fast rule when working on any quilting project: ***Begin everything in the center and work toward the outside edges***. When you start in the center, any excess fabric will be pushed to the edges as you work, instead of bunching up in the middle.

Before starting a project, read through the following instructions:

1. Choose a project. Determine the finished size it will need to be.

2. Make the allotted number of squares.

3. When laying out the proposed design, try to distribute the squares for good visual appeal. For example, if you have two squares that are "busier" than the others, do not place them next to each other. Mix them in with simpler squares. Another example of this principle involves colored squares. Try not to place all the dark squares together; instead, intersperse them with lighter ones. When the designs in certain squares face in different directions, take that into consideration when placing them in the finished project.

4. Before you actually start stitching a project together, lay it out where you can view it for a time. Study the layout and make changes; study it further and make any more changes. Ask others' opinions, and then, when all possibilities have been exhausted, start assembling the project.

5. If sashing is to be part of the design, add it now.

6. If borders are to be used, stitch them on now. When you are using two or more border rows, add pizzazz to your project by varying the widths. For example, in a 3-row border, the first row could be 2 inches, the second 4 inches, and the third 1½ inches. (You would **not** want to make them 3 inches, 2 inches, and 1 inch—that would be too set.)

7. Transfer quilting designs onto the assembled quilt top. (See column 2, "Marking the Quilting Designs.")

8. The size of the finished project will determine the way you put together the quilt back. For a large project, you will probably need to stitch two widths of material together. Using a ⅝-inch seam allowance, do that now.

9. Lay the quilt back, wrong side up, on the floor. Tape it down with masking tape.

10. Now, spread quilt batting on the quilt back. Tape it down as well.

11. Next, lay the finished quilt top, right side up, on the batting and tape it down. You now have a quilting sandwich.

12. ***Starting in the center and working toward the outside edges***, baste, baste, and baste a bit more. Pinning may also be very helpful.

13. Use a quilting frame or large hoop to hold work taut while quilting.

Marking the Quilting Designs

It is easier to transfer quilting designs to the project top **before** the sandwich of top, batting, and backing has been basted together.

1. Make the project top.

2. Choose the quilting designs for the entire project. A lot of quilting adds interest and serves to reinforce and strengthen the work. The smaller quilting patterns on pages 109–111 give plenty of design choices.

3. To transfer quilting designs to the project top, make a template and trace around it with a quilt marker, or use dressmaker carbon between design and the top. Start tracing in upper left corner, following the design around until you are back at the starting point.

Design Tip: For a project featuring lighthouse squares, you can enhance your work by quilting a dory or other nautical item, placing it partially in the lighthouse square and partially on the surrounding border. This gives the project a striking, ornamental uniqueness.

Quilting Stitches

Two different stitches are generally used in quilt making. The first is a simple running stitch, used for hand-piecing patchwork and decorative quilting. The second is the slip-stitch used for invisibly attaching appliqué pieces. The slip-stitch has already been explained in the "Achievable Appliqué" chapter, page 8.

To make the running stitch, you simply weave the needle in and out, taking short, evenly spaced stitches. The resulting row of stitching looks like this:

- -

When you are quilting a project, you, the quilter, will decide on the complexity of the decorative stitching. Each lighthouse square in this book includes quilting tips for that particular design. Many of them start by directing you to outline quilt around certain pieces. Outline quilting simply means to stitch close to the contours of that piece. This type of stitching brings out the design without competing with it. You may also decide to work your quilting stitches into the shapes of stars, boats, shells, or any of the other decorative motifs shown in the "Just Plain Quilting" chapter.

Gridline Quilting

The items pictured in this book mostly feature outline quilting, though in a few places I also stitched a pattern of parallel diagonal lines. You might prefer to do your quilting in an even grid rather than simply outlining the appliqué pieces or stitching shells, waves, anchors, or other motifs, so here are directions for stitching an allover gridline pattern.

Use masking tape to assist you with the grid. Choose a measurement (such as ¾ inch) to use between quilting lines, and use that width of tape.

For a diamond grid: Place a straight length of tape on the sandwich with one edge of the tape going from one corner to the opposite corner. Quilt along one edge of the tape, then the other. Next, pick up the tape and align one edge against the quilting line just completed. Quilt along the other edge of the tape. Proceed in this manner until the entire area is quilted with parallel lines. (When one piece of tape loses its sticking ability, start a fresh piece.) Make the cross-hatching by aligning a length of tape from one of the two remaining corners to the opposite corner, crossing the already stitched lines at a right angle. Proceed as described above.

For a square grid: Work the first line of quilting across the center of the patch from side to side rather than from corner to corner. First, measure halfway up one side of the patch, then do the same on the opposite side. Place your masking tape along this center line. Quilt along one edge of the tape, then the other. Next, move the tape so one edge is against the quilting line just completed. Quilt along the other edge. Proceed in this manner until the entire area has been quilted with parallel lines. (When one piece of tape loses its sticking ability, start a fresh piece.) Begin the cross-hatching by placing the first length of masking tape across the center of the square at a right angle to the already stitched lines. Proceed as described above.

Making Continuous Bias Binding

Most projects, especially large quilts, are bound with bias binding. Completed projects look more polished when bound with matching fabric. To make yards of continuous bias binding, follow these simple steps:

1. Draw a diagonal line on the wrong side of your fabric square (top sketch).

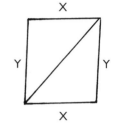

2. Cut along this line to make 2 triangles. Match the edges marked X in the top sketch and stitch the triangles together along that side, using a ¼-inch seam allowance. Press the seam allowance to one side. Mark parallel lines along the bias every 1¼ inches (middle sketch).

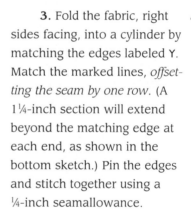

3. Fold the fabric, right sides facing, into a cylinder by matching the edges labeled Y. Match the marked lines, *offsetting the seam by one row.* (A 1¼-inch section will extend beyond the matching edge at each end, as shown in the bottom sketch.) Pin the edges and stitch together using a ¼-inch seamallowance.

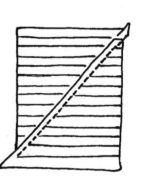

4. Starting at one end, begin cutting on the marked lines as though peeling an apple in one continuous strip. Press the strip. Fold it in half, wrong sides facing, and press again. Now, open up the strip and fold one edge in to the center crease. Press. Repeat with the other side.

Congratulations! You have made your own bias tape! A 36-inch square of material yields approximately 13½ yards of tape.

Smaller Projects

Wall hangings, lap quilts, table runners, and other small projects can be made in any size. Long, narrow hangings displayed on a door look terrific. Just measure the spot where a project is to be displayed, pick out a design, and follow the instructions for any quilting project. For small projects you can either use a quilting hoop or simply hold the sandwich of top, batting, and backing in your hand as you do the quilt stitching.

Hangings may encompass one quilt square to which several rows of sashing and/or borders have been added. *Remember:* When two or more border rows are added, vary the row widths to add visual interest.

This handsome wall hanging is a good example of how appliqué and "just plain quilting" techniques work well together. It features a single lighthouse appliqué square. The inner border pieces are quilted with seashell motifs. Outline-quilted stars decorate the wider outer border. The small appliqué squares on the outermost corners were made from the buoy quilting pattern. (Many of the quilting patterns on pages 99–108 work equally well as templates for appliqué pieces.)

Coasters

To make a quilted-design coaster set, follow the "Preparing the Square" directions in the "Just Plain Quilting" chapter (page 98). *To make an appliquéd coaster set,* follow directions in the "Achievable Appliqué" chapter (page 7). Appliqué design coasters can be made using either the slip-stitching or fusible webbing method.

After completing a coaster set, trim the edges evenly and bind with bias binding (directions on page 11), or fold under the edges and slip-stitch around.

A small buoy and starfish were used on this coaster worked in "just plain quilting."

Picture-Perfect Pillows

Making pillows is not difficult. Just follow these directions carefully. Stuff the completed pillow with fiberfill or a purchased pillow form. These directions are for a pillow with no zipper. If you want a zipper, you will need to insert it into the pillow back *before* stitching the pillow front and back together. (You must use a pillow form, not fiberfill, for a zippered pillow.)

After you have made the quilt square for your pillow top, you will need to decide whether your pillow will have a plain edge, a corded edge, or a ruffle. Directions for all three styles follow.

Making a Pillow

l. Make the quilt square that will be the pillow top.

2. Cut a fabric square the same size as this top for the pillow back.

3. If your pillow will have a ruffle or a corded edge, prepare the ruffle or cord, following Steps R1 through R6 or C1 through C4 below. For a pillow with plain edges, proceed with step 4.

4. With right sides together, and using a ¼-inch seam allowance, stitch pillow back to pillow top on three sides, also stitching in a little way on each end of the fourth side. *Note:* If you have inserted a zipper, stitch completely around *all four* sides of pillow.

5. Turn right side out and press.

6. Stuff pillow with fiberfill or insert pillow form. Turn under ¼ inch on the open edge of back piece and blind-stitch the opening closed.

To Add a Ruffle

R1. To make the ruffle, prepare a length of fabric that measures twice the total length of the four sides of the pillow top. For example, a 12-inch-square pillow will need a length of material that is 12 times 4 times 2 (12 x 4 = 48 x 2 = 96 inches). How wide should the fabric be? Double the desired ruffle width and add 1 inch for the seam allowance. For a 2-inch ruffle, the calculation would be: 2 x 2 = 4 + 1 = 5 inches.

R2. Next, stitch the short ends together, forming one continuous piece. Fold this in half lengthwise with wrong sides together, and press.

R3. Using the longest machine stitch, stitch two basting rows along the unfinished edge. Stitch first row ¼ inch from edge and second row ½ inch from edge.

R4. Divide the ruffle into four sections by folding it in half and then in half again. Pin each section to a corner of the pillow top on the right side. Using the basting threads, pull the gathers to fit, evenly distributing the fullness around the ruffle.

R5. Pin and stitch ruffle to right side of pillow top, using a ¼-inch seam allowance. (The stitching should be done *between* the basting rows on the ruffle, as close as possible to the first row of basting.) After completely stitching ruffle to pillow top, pull out basting stitches; this will help the gathers to lie evenly.

R6. Assemble the pillow as described in Steps 4 through 6 under "Making a Pillow," keeping the ruffle on the inside of the "envelope" as you stitch around the edges to join the pillow top and back together.

To Add a Corded Edge

C1. Cut a 1-inch width of fabric on the bias. The strip needs to be long enough to wrap all the way around the edge of the pillow, plus 1 inch. Cut a length of cable cord long enough to wrap all the way around the pillow *without* the extra inch.

C2. With the fabric strip right-side down, place the cable cord along center of strip. Bring the raw edges together, encasing the cable cord. Using a zipper foot, stitch close to cording. Trim the edge of the finished cording piece to measure ¼ inch from stitching to the raw edge.

C3. Baste cording to pillow top.

C4. Assemble the pillow as described in Steps 4 through 6 under "Making a Pillow," keeping the cord on the inside of the "envelope" as you stitch around the edges to join the pillow top and back together.

You have just completed a picture-perfect pillow! This is comparable to making a sentence. For a statement, make several pillows to group on a bed or sofa.

Timeless Tote Bag

Totes are good for traveling, carrying books or toys, or organizing tasks. What could be better than a tote with a quilted pocket?

This simple tote bag consists of one straight length of material and two handles. It can be lined, if you wish, but works equally well without a lining.

Materials Needed

1¼ yards heavy fabric
12-inch quilted square for pocket
Optional: Decorative fabric for trim on handles

Cut

One 18" x 35" rectangle
Two 3" x 22" strips for straps
Optional: Two 1" x 22" strips for trim on handles

Making the Tote Bag

1. Fold fabric rectangle in half, right sides facing, with short ends meeting.

2. Tuck folded end up into middle of bag for 2½ inches, as shown at right. Stitch through all thicknesses.

3. Press under ¼ inch on each long side of handle pieces. Bring pressed edges together, wrong sides facing. Topstitch close to edge on both handles.

4. Next, topstitch along folded edge of each handle. (If you wish to add trim to the center of each handle, now is the time to do it. Press under ¼ inch on long sides of each trim strip. Align strip down center of each handle and top-stitch along both edges.)

5. Turn the bag inside out. Now, measure an equal distance from each side seam of bag and pin the handles to the inside upper edge of the bag (see the sketch at left).

6. Press a 1-inch hem around the top of the bag. Fold under ¼ inch along the raw edge and stitch (bottom sketch).

7. Bring the handles up to top of bag. Then, topstitch around top of bag, catching in the handles as you go.

8. Finally, turn the bag right side out, position and pin your quilted square to front of tote bag, pin, and blind-stitch along three sides to form a pocket. You may wish to sew a piece of Velcro or a snap in the middle of the fourth side for a pocket closure.

Put your latest project into the bag or present it to a friend as a gift.

Always sign and date your quilting projects.
Use embroidery floss or a permanent marker.

▣ Maine Lighthouses in Appliqué
(With a Bit of Patchwork Here and There)

The Keepers and Their Lights

The sea will always be a mesmerizing presence, drawing us to its beauty, its solitude, its mystery. While the sea can be tranquil, it can be treacherous as well. Those who have always known the ocean cannot be far from it for long. The pull of the salt water is as strong as the pull of the tides. There is no escaping it. What can possibly match that smell? How do you replicate the feel of salt spray against your skin? What else can replenish your soul as you simply gaze at it?

The sea is a narcotic, compelling men to leave both land and loved ones, to pledge their allegiance to her waters. An enticing mistress, the sea draws men under her spell while constantly demanding the utmost respect from those who become entranced by her magnetism.

It was this human desire to have a relationship with the ocean and the subsequent need for safe passage that inspired the creation of lighthouses. Lighthouses have been in existence since before recorded time. The original wooden structures built here on our Atlantic coast were unable to bear the worst of nature's fury. Wood was gradually replaced by granite, iron, brick, and rubblestone, all of which have withstood the test of time.

Rubblestone, a combination of area stones and rock chipped from nearby ledges, was used for the earliest towers because the fledgling government's treasury had little money to spare. These initial structures were cone shaped with a three-foot-thick base, tapering to a two-foot thickness at the top, offering maximum resistance to the onslaught of a boiling sea. Neither size, shape, nor building material was important to the mariner—only the reliability of the light cutting the blackness mattered to them.

Although lighthouses are usually associated with storm-tossed ships and dark, cloudless nights, these beacons are also necessary on starry, moonlit nights and bright, sunny days. Dangerous rocks are permanent, and seas can run heavy even when no storm is fermenting.

By day, lighthouses are visual landmarks, each unique in its appearance. After dark, each tower has its own signal, identifiable by a fixed or flashing light, a given number of flashes, the interval between the flashes, and the color of the light. The height above sea level, the distance the beacon reaches, and the strength of that beacon are of the utmost significance.

Before the advent of modern technology, mariners predicted weather by watching seabirds, feeling the air around them, observing a ring around the moon, and by paying attention to wind direction and sky color. "Red skies in the morning, sailors take warning. Red skies at night, sailors' delight." Yet ships were often caught unaware of impending storms. Violent weather could arrive with little warning.

Today, mariners listen to scientifically detailed weather reports while still adhering to many old-time weather predictors. Most mariners come from seafaring families—could there be a weather gene passed down through seafaring generations?

Along Maine's coastline, lighthouses were welcoming beacons to ships and coastal communities. Mariners felt safer knowing there were reliable lights. After lighthouses became permanent fixtures, fewer ships ran aground on rocky ledges and countless lives were spared.

Those who operated the lighthouses during the early years were selfless people, often exhibiting courage beyond comprehension. They were sometimes called "wickies," and though that sounds like such a sissy name, being a light keeper was certainly not for the faint of heart. Island duty was the most arduous. When the wind whipped the surrounding sea to a seething froth, keepers could only wait out the tempest as they battled to keep the lights burning. Only the stouthearted lasted for long periods of time on these rugged outposts.

Light keepers were not always men; sometimes women tended the lights. Duty on many stations was lonely, tough, and demanding for all family members. Occasionally, even keepers' children were called to duty.

One such offspring was Abbie Burgess. Abbie's father was in charge of the dual light towers at Matinicus Rock. Duty on the most isolated station along the Maine coast was difficult at best. On calm days the water swirled and sloshed around the rocky perimeter. On stormy days the ferocious sea pummeled the island.

Abbie's mother was an invalid, her three sisters were very young, and her older brother worked away from the island. That left Abbie to assist her father with his chores on "The Rock." She routinely filled lamps, trimmed wicks, and cleaned lenses.

In January 1856, Samuel Burgess left the station to replenish their supplies. While he was gone, a tremendous gale hit the coast, and the seas continued to rage for weeks after, hampering his return for a month. Teenaged Abbie became the light keeper in his absence.

On January 19, crashing seas flooded the house and swallowed anything not firmly attached to The Rock's thirty-two granite acres. Abbie rescued the family's chickens moments before the storm demolished the hen house. Realizing the waters were rising higher with each tide, Abbie moved her mother and sisters to safety in the tower. Despite hurricane-force winds, sleet, snow, and bone-chilling cold, Abbie tended the lights. Never once did the third-order Fresnel lens fail to beam seaward. And remember, there were two separate towers, each with its own light to maintain as a gyrating sea attempted to foil her every move.

The scene was repeated the following year. This time Abbie was in charge for a mere twenty-one days, but by the time her father and brother returned, the daily rations had shrunk to one egg and one cup of corn meal.

Samuel was eventually fired as the keeper and replaced by Captain John Grant. Abbie and her father remained at The Rock to familiarize the new keeper with the lighthouse responsibilities.

During that time, Abbie and John's son, Isaac, fell in love and exchanged wedding vows. Abbie gave birth to their four children on the island. Their two-year-old daughter, Bessie, died there, and is the only person ever to be buried at Matinicus Rock. Abbie died at the age of fifty-three, having spent forty of those years assisting in the upkeep of lighthouses. The United States Coast Guard cutter *Abbie Burgess* is named after her, a fitting honor for the courageous woman whose legendary life is indelibly blended with the surrounding waters.

Each Maine lighthouse comes with its own story. Most are ordinary. Many are dramatic. Some have romantic overtones. With the advancement of technology, the beacons were gradually automated. Some ceased to shine entirely, demolished in the name of economics. A few decommissioned lights were destroyed by vandals.

Fortunately, people began to realize the need to protect these historic landmarks. Many have been restored by individuals or taken over by towns or organizations. Some now house museums. Thank the mariners' guiding stars, most of the towers still survive to remind us of Maine's rich maritime history.

LIGHTHOUSE DESIGNS For Quilters

Patricia A. Aho

12 MAINE LIGHTHOUSES / APPLIQUÉ & PATCHWORK DESIGNS

Down East Books

For my loving family—
those who were, those who are,
and those yet to be . . .

Smell the sea, observe its ever-changing face,
touch its cold wetness,
taste its salty brine, and let its sound
soothe your being.

I owe special thanks to my longtime friend,
Earl "Bud" Warren, renowned Maine historian,
for answering my questions about
the factual information about lighthouses.

And thanks to Karin Womer, my editor,
who followed the rules of quilting by exercising
persistance, perseverance, and patience
throughout the development of this book.

Copyright © 2005 by Patricia A. Aho. All rights reserved.

ISBN: 0-89272-599-0   13-digit: 978-089272-599-1

LCCN: 2004105097

Printed at Versa Press, E. Peoria, Ill.

5   4   3   2   1

DOWN EAST BOOKS
A DIVISION OF DOWN EAST ENTERPRISE, INC.,
PUBLISHER OF DOWN EAST, THE MAGAZINE OF MAINE

BOOK ORDERS: **1-800-685-7962**
www.downeastbooks.com

MAINE LIGHTHOUSE THROW

A combination of applique, patchwork, and plain quilting squares makes a nicely balanced, not too busy ensemble for a throw or wall hanging. Here, eight Maine Lighthouse squares alternate with squares worked in "just plain quilting" (p. 98). Patchwork Schooner squares (p. 92) fill the corners, and another patchwork motif, Mariner's Compass (p. 94) occupies the center square. The squares are joined together with no sashing strips between.

BOON ISLAND LIGHT QUILT SQUARE
Crazy-quilt blocks of color create an interesting rocky shoreline effect in the foreground. A puffy appliqué cloud floats in the sky. (Directions are on p. 33.)

BURNT ISLAND LIGHT QUILT SQUARE
On this example, subtle cloud shapes are worked in outline stitching only. Quilting stitches trace the edge of each appliquéd piece. (Directions are on p. 36.)

CUCKOLDS LIGHT QUILT SQUARE (above)

Only a few appliqué pieces are needed for this bold design. On this example, diagonal lines of quilting add textural interest on the brown rocky ground area. (Directions are on p. 41.)

DICE HEAD LIGHT QUILT SQUARE (right)

The branch pattern and pine tree outlines worked in quilting stitches add another layer of interest to the overall design of the square. (Directions are on p. 44.)

GOOSE ROCKS LIGHT QUILT SQUARE
Wave patterns are quilted in the water area of this nicely balanced square. Outline quilting frames the other appliqué pieces. (Directions are on p. 49.)

THREE-SQUARE TABLE RUNNER
Here a Dice Head Light appliqué square (p. 44) is flanked by two "just plain quilting" squares worked in snowflake and star motifs (pps. 103 and 82).

WALL HANGING, GRINDLE POINT LIGHT QUILT SQUARE

A creative broad border can turn a single lighthouse square into a dramatic wall hanging. Here, the foreground of Grindle Point Light square (p. 52) is quilted in parallel diagonal lines, while stitched lines of waves add texture to the water area. Appliquéd lobster buoys (p. 109) anchor the corners. The inner border pieces are quilted with shell motifs (p. 110), and quilted stars (p. 82) enliven the outer border.

KENNEBEC RIVER RANGE LIGHTS QUILT SQUARE
(Left) This square is unusual because it shows
two lighthouse towers. Layers of trees offer
an opportunity to experiment with com-
patible fabric prints. Branch patterns (p. 111)
stitched in the trees add even more interest.
(Directions are on p. 56.)

MARSHALL POINT LIGHT QUILT SQUARE (Below)
The ramp's strong diagonal lines add drama
to this view of one of Maine's handsomest and
most accessible lighthouses. (Directions are
on p. 61.)

MONHEGAN ISLAND LIGHT QUILT SQUARE

Whether to add clouds to any lighthouse square, and whether to work them in appliqué or outline stitching is a matter of personal choice. This example shows both. (Directions are on p. 66.)

ROCKLAND BREAKWATER LIGHT QUILT SQUARE

Although no one has lived there for years, the attractive and historic keeper's house still stands at this Maine light station perched at the end of a mile-long breakwater. (Directions are on p. 70.)

SEGUIN ISLAND LIGHT QUILT SQUARE

This unusual view focuses on just the top of the lighthouse tower. Details of the railing and glass-sided lantern room are worked with embroidery floss. Sunset colors in the sky would make a beautiful variation of this design, and shapes of soaring sea gulls could be quilted in the sky. (Directions are on p. 74.)

WEST QUODDY HEAD LIGHT QUILT SQUARE

The red and white stripes make Maine's easternmost light distinctive—and its quilt square fun to assemble. (Directions are on p. 78.)

THOSE PESKY CROWS
A stylized lighthouse graces this whimsical wall hanging worked in blanket stitch appliqué. Continuing the playful theme, the lantern at the top of the lighthouse tower sports a star-shaped yellow button. (Directions are on p. 84)

MARINER'S COMPASS QUILT SQUARE

Paired light and dark shades lend a three-dimensional effect to this boldly geometric design. The compass rose works beautifully as the center for a larger piece, such as the throw shown on page 17, or in a single-square project such as a pillow or tote bag. (Directions are on p. 94.)

PATCHWORK SCHOONER QUILT SQUARE

In patchwork, the complex shapes of hull and sails are simplified to right triangles, yet we still instantly recognize this as a proud sailing ship. This example shows a vessel with dark (tanbark) sails, but the square could also be made with white sails against a darker sky. (Directions are on p. 92.)

PILLOW WITH RUFFLED EDGE AND APPLIQUE STARS

Decorative buttons add a festive touch. On this pillow, the stars are worked in blanket stitch appliqué (p. 8). Directions for pillows are on p. 13.

PILLOW WITH CORDED EDGE AND QUILTED DESIGN

Most of the "just plain quilting" designs can be used to make a classy pillow top. This ensemble features the Three-Masted Schooner (p. 104), Large Crab (p. 100), and Scallop (p. 101). Directions for pillows are are on p. 13.

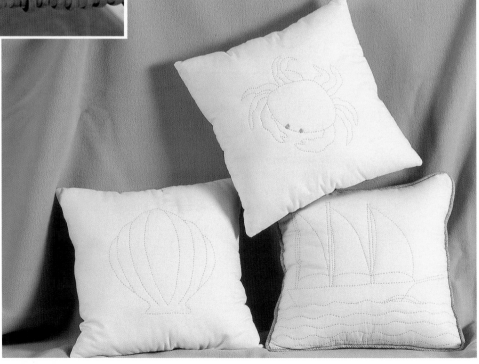

THE BEAUTY OF STITCHING

(Top left) Coasters (p. 12) can feature outline-stitched designs worked with thread in a contrasting color. This example is edged with bias binding (p. 11).

(Above) Carefully stitched quilting makes the back of the wall hanging shown on p. 32 as beautiful as the front. In this corner we can see the various border quilting motifs and the outline stitching around the appliqué pieces in the Monhegan Island Light Square.

(Bottom left) Quilting designs can often be effectively combined in a square. Here we see the large dory (p. 106) together with rows of a wave motif (p. 102).

SQUARE WITH QUILTED SNOWFLAKE
The crisp, bold snowflake motif (p. 103) is a design just for quilting.

COASTERS WITH NAUTICAL MOTIFS
Quilting designs from pages 99 through 111 can also be used for appliqué work. These plain-edge coasters (p. 12) were made with fusible appliqué plus decorative blanket stitching (p. 8).

TOTE BAG WITH KALEIDOSCOPIC FRESNEL QUILT SQUARE

Inspired by the prismatic colors created by a lighthouse's multifaceted Fresnel lens,
this patchwork design works beautifully in either pastel or bright color combinations.
Although it looks complicated, the array of colors is actually simple to assemble.
(Tote bag directions, p. 14. Kaleidoscopic Fresnel quilt square directions, p. 89.)

FOUR-SQUARE MAINE LIGHTHOUSE WALL HANGING

Maine Lighthouse squares are framed by borders and sashes that look plain at first glance. A closer look reveals many interesting smaller quilting patterns from pages 108 through 110. Notice how the appliquéd clouds (p. 103) add a three-dimensional effect and help unify the layout.

Boon Island Light

*B*oon Island Light is located on perhaps the most danger-ous outcropping of rocks along this country's eastern seaboard. So many ships were wrecked on those treacherous ledges that the fishermen of York kept a barrel filled with life-saving provisions (called a boon) on the island specifically for shipwrecked sailors. Begun in the late 1600s, this practice continued until the completion of the final light tower in 1800. Eventually, the rocky outcropping off the shore of York became known as Boon Island.

The original wooden tower lasted for five years before it was demolished by a violent storm. A stone tower, built in 1831, was also destroyed. The present structure, boasting a five-wick lantern, first beamed its light nineteen miles sea-ward on New Year's Day of 1855. This larger, stronger bastion was constructed of massive, hand-cut granite blocks, with a twenty-five-foot base tapering to twelve feet.

Rising 133 feet skyward, Boon Island Light is the tallest in Maine. On a calm day, the seven-hundred-foot length of rocky terrain supporting it protrudes a mere fourteen feet above the sea. Only eight miles off the coast of Maine's first city, the craggy island may as well be on another planet dur-ing a storm, as shrieking winds and raging surf completely cover it.

Living on this godforsaken rock was lonely, and most keepers lasted but a short while. Keeper William Williams was the exception. During the winter of 1888, a storm forced Williams and his crew to take refuge in the top of the tower for three days. Still, he and his wife chose to stay on Boon Island for twenty-seven years.

Until the advent of radio, carrier pigeons were Boon Island's only means of communicating with civilization. It took the pigeons ten minutes to fly to the mainland. Since birds do not fly during storms, a man stuck on Boon Island during violent weather was left to his own devices.

Weathering storms was not the only frightening part of a Boon Island light keeper's job. Another daunting task was painting the top of the lantern tower. In the early days, the only safety device was a rope thrown over the tower dome, looped around, and made fast to the ball and lightning rod. All activity stopped and apprehensive eyes turned heavenward as the black paint was being applied.

Destructive storms were not exclusively a problem of the early years. A tremendous storm hit the Maine coast in 1978. This storm generated seventy-foot waves that smashed into Boon Island with unyielding force. The lighthouse's living quarters were completely destroyed, and the two keepers sought refuge by climbing the 130 narrow, winding steps to the top of the light tower. The tower stood firm, despite the fact the entire island was submerged under five feet of water. Thundering waves beat their persistent rhythm as screeching winds plucked the support wires, creating an eerie tuneless rhythm. Finally, a Coast Guard helicopter rescued the keepers from their lofty perch.

Through years of pleasant weather and terrifying storms, keepers kept the light burning in the Boon Island tower. The second-order Fresnel flashed its white light every five seconds. After the 1978 storm, the light was automated. The tower was outfitted with solar power in 1993.

Some pictures of Boon Island Light make the tower look forlorn, invoking a desolate feeling. This quilt design replicates a view of the tower standing tall and proud, a perspective that seems to say, "I have stood the test of time; I have weathered the best and the worst nature has thrown at me. I am still standing, a symbol of Yankee fortitude, perseverance, and longevity."

The sky-pattern fabric forms the base of this square. A collage of pieces appliquéd in a crazy patchwork design depicts the rocky ledge.

Materials Needed

Fabrics:

12½" x 12½" piece for sky
Light gray for tower
Black for tower top, trim, door, and windows
Yellow for light
Small pieces in a mix of colors and patterns
　　for rocks
White for clouds
3¾" x 12½" piece of muslin for backing of rocks

Black embroidery floss

Assembling the Square

Read through all instructions below before beginning this square. You will assemble the crazy-quilt foreground rocks first, then the rest of the square.

1. Before starting to piece the crazy quilt island, measure 2½ inches up from the bottom left side of the muslin and 3½ inches up on the right side. Draw a line between these points. Use this guideline as the imaginary top of the rock ledge. Place cloth pieces for the tumbled rocks approximately along the line, making an uneven edge.

2. Starting at the lower right side of the muslin, pin a piece of "rock" cloth to the background. Stitch in place. Next, place the right side of the next rock over the first piece. Stitch in place along its right-hand edge. Fold this piece forward (right-side showing), finger press in place, and continue with the next rock. (As you arrange the rest of the rocks, it might occasionally be easier to turn a seam under and slip-stitch it in place.)

3. Work crazy-quilt rocks across the entire width of muslin, leaving top seam open. After completing the rock ledge, trim excess muslin from top. Turn under the top seam allowance and baste. Now, matching the bottom and side edges, pin the sides and bottom of the assembled rock

QUILT SQUARE. FOR COLOR PHOTO, SEE P. 18.

ledge piece to the sky background, but do not secure the ledge top to the background square just yet. Set aside.

4. Prepare pieces for appliqué (p. 7 "How to Appliqué," steps 1–4). Note that there is no need to fold and baste the top and bottom edges of the tower—they will be overlapped by other pieces.

5. Fit and pin the tower behind the top of the rock ledge. Baste tower and top of ledge to background.

6. Pin windows and door in place on tower. Baste.

7. Pin tower top, light, tower trim, and clouds in place. Baste.

8. Slip-stitch all pieces to background. Press.

9. Referring to the Boon Island Light quilt square photograph, use 2 strands of embroidery floss to embroider all trim. Press finished square.

If the square is to be part of a larger project such as a bedcover or wall hanging, set it aside until you assemble the project.

For a single-square project such as a tote bag or pillow, make a sandwich of completed lighthouse square, batting, and backing. Baste. Complete your project according to the directions in the "Projects, Projects, Projects" chapter.

Quilting Suggestions

Outline quilt around the tower, clouds, and each individual rock.

Trace or make photocopy at 100% size. Cut one of each unless otherwise noted.

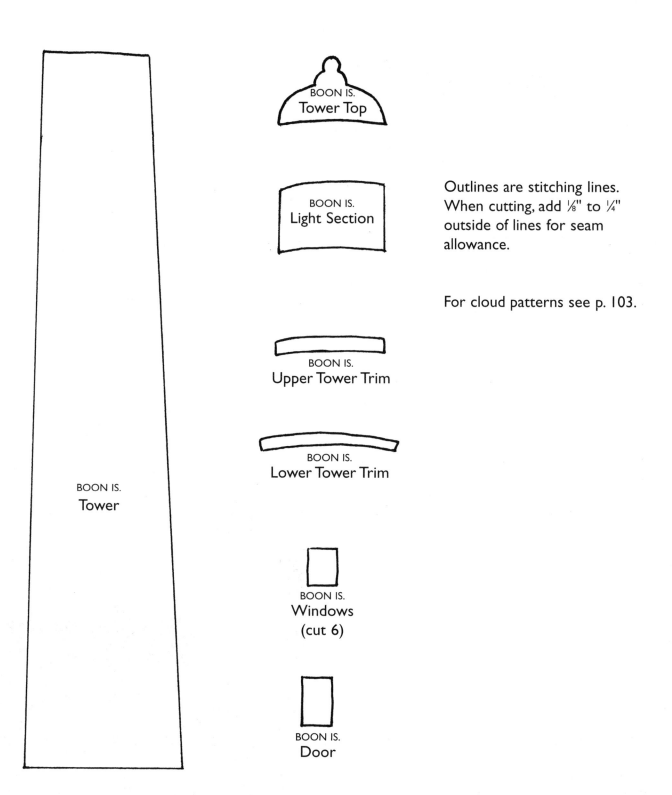

BOON IS.
Tower Top

BOON IS.
Light Section

BOON IS.
Upper Tower Trim

BOON IS.
Lower Tower Trim

BOON IS.
Tower

BOON IS.
Windows
(cut 6)

BOON IS.
Door

Outlines are stitching lines.
When cutting, add ⅛" to ¼"
outside of lines for seam
allowance.

For cloud patterns see p. 103.

Burnt Island Light

*M*aine boasts more than one Burnt Island. This one lies at the west entrance to Boothbay Harbor and can be seen from the eastern side as well. Constructed in 1821, the lighthouse here is one of Maine's earliest. It originally consisted of a 30-foot stone tower and a wooden keeper's house. Stone towers needed a yearly whitewashing, usually done on a late spring day when the westerly wind could speed the drying.

The house on Burnt Island was replaced in 1857 with a larger dwelling. Later additions included a walkway from house to tower, a boathouse, and an oil house. The final addition, in 1895, was a tower for the thousand-pound fog bell. During the mid-nineteenth century, the tower was enlarged to accommodate a fourth-order Fresnel lens with four bull's-eyes. In 1888 a dark sector was added, and in 1892 the now familiar red flashing light with white sectors was adopted.

Burnt Island was the last Maine light station to convert from kerosene to electricity, in1962. It was also among the last lights to be automated (1989). Maine Master Gardener volunteers are presently creating gardens on the grounds.

Materials Needed

Fabrics:

8" x 12½" sky background piece
5" x 12½" grass piece
Gray for ledges and rocks
White for tower and outbuilding
4 green prints for trees—1 light, 1 medium, 2 dark
Red for outbuilding roof and tower light
Black for tower top, section piece, and trim
Dark print for outbuilding window

Black embroidery floss for tower trim

Assembling the Square

You will first assemble the foreground (lower portion of square), then the sky, trees, and tower (upper portion).

1. Prepare pieces for appliqué (p. 7, "How to Appliqué," steps 1–4), referring to the photograph to determine which edges to leave flat because they will be overlapped by other pieces.

2. Baste the front ledge to the bottom of the grass piece, matching bottoms and sides. Baste the tower front ledge to the top left of grass piece. Place rocks randomly on the grass and baste in place.

QUILT SQUARE. FOR COLOR PHOTOGRAPH, SEE P. 18.

3. Arrange and pin tree sections to sky background, matching bottoms and sides. Put light green in back, medium green in middle, and dark green in front. Baste.

4. Pin tree to left of sky background, matching sides and bottoms. Baste.

5. Pin tower in place, matching bottoms. Pin light section, tower top, and tower trim to sky background. When satisfied with placement, baste pieces in place.

6. Baste outbuilding and roof to sky background. Baste window to outbuilding.

7. Using a ¼-inch seam allowance, stitch sky piece to ledge/grass piece.

8. Slip-stitch all pieces to background. Press.

9. Referring to the Burnt Island Light quilt square photograph, use 2 strands of embroidery floss to embroider all trim. Press finished square.

If the square is to be part of a larger project such as a bedcover or wall hanging, set it aside until you assemble the project.

For a single-square project such as a tote bag or pillow, make a sandwich of completed lighthouse square, batting, and backing. Baste. Complete your project according to the directions in the "Projects, Projects, Projects" chapter.

Quilting Suggestions

Outline quilt around each piece. Quilt the panes in the outbuilding window. You can also quilt shingle rows on the outbuilding roof and branches on the trees.

---------------------- **BURNT ISLAND LIGHT / Pattern Pieces** ----------------------

BURNT IS.
Tower Trim

Outlines are stitching lines. When cutting, add ⅛" to ¼" outside of lines for seam allowance.

BURNT IS.
Roof

BURNT IS.
Tower

Trace or photocopy at 100% size. Cut one of each.

BURNT IS.
Window

BURNT IS.
Outbuilding

Trace or make photocopy at 100% size. Cut one of each.
Solid lines are stitching lines. When cutting, add ⅛" to ¼" outside of lines for seam allowance.
Dashed lines are cutting lines for edges that will align with edge of quilt square.

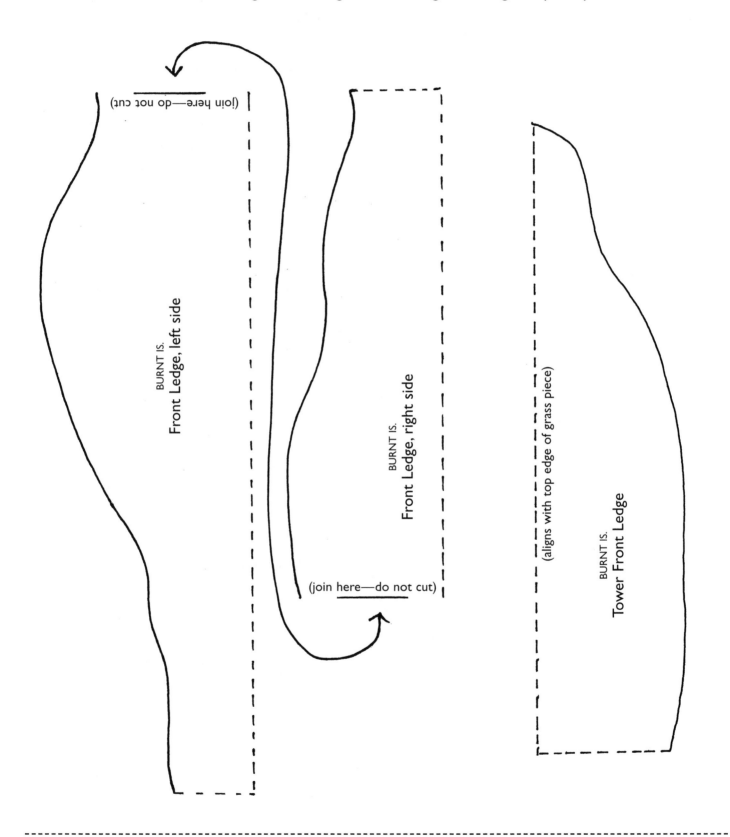

(join here—do not cut)

BURNT IS.
Front Ledge, left side

(join here—do not cut)

BURNT IS.
Front Ledge, right side

(aligns with top edge of grass piece)

BURNT IS.
Tower Front Ledge

Trace or make photocopy at 100% size. Cut one of each.

Solid lines are stitching lines. When cutting, add ⅛" to ¼" outside of lines for seam allowance.

Dashed lines are cutting lines for edges that will align with edge of quilt square.

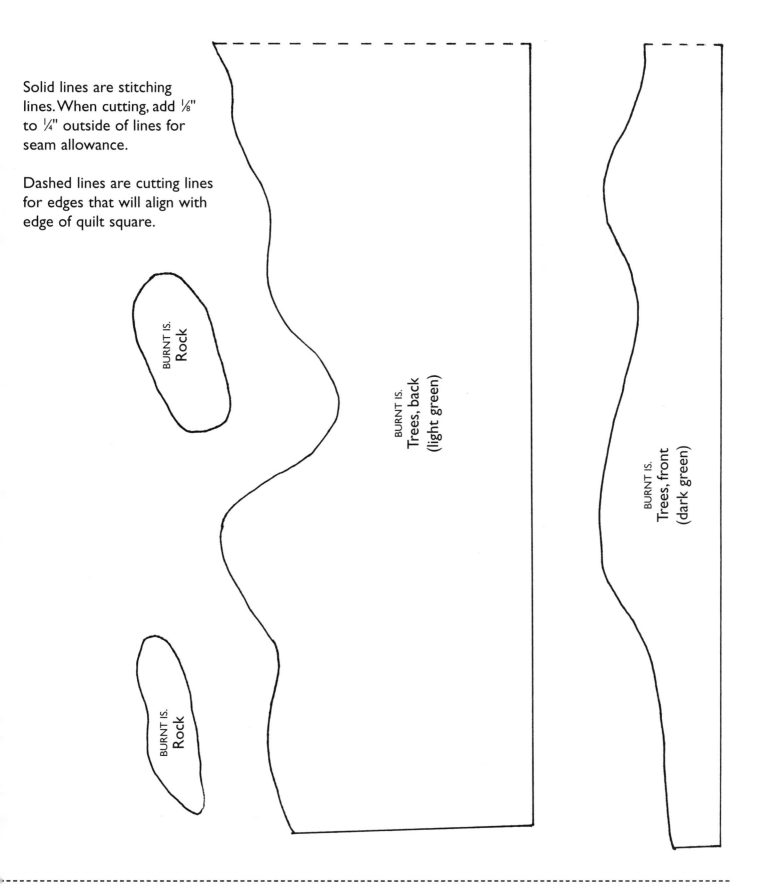

BURNT IS.
Rock

BURNT IS.
Rock

BURNT IS.
Trees, back
(light green)

BURNT IS.
Trees, front
(dark green)

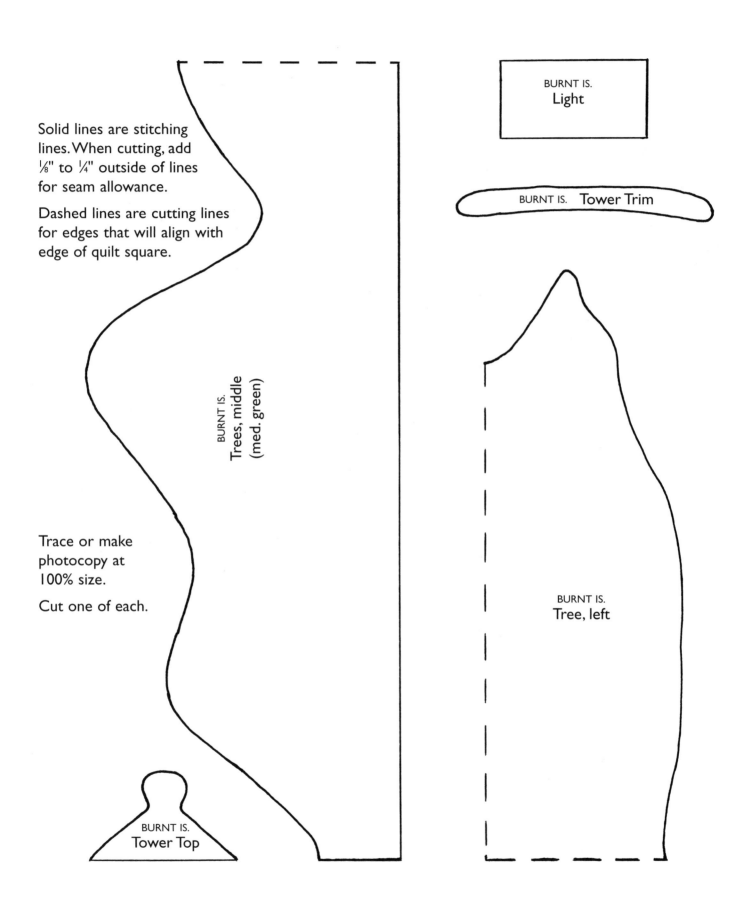

Solid lines are stitching lines. When cutting, add $\frac{1}{8}$" to $\frac{1}{4}$" outside of lines for seam allowance.

Dashed lines are cutting lines for edges that will align with edge of quilt square.

Trace or make photocopy at 100% size.

Cut one of each.

BURNT IS.
Light

BURNT IS. **Tower Trim**

BURNT IS.
Trees, middle
(med. green)

BURNT IS.
Tree, left

BURNT IS.
Tower Top

The Cuckolds Light

*T*he Cuckolds—there's a name to raise from the throat. My Uncle Weston Thompson was light keeper there in the 1940s. He and Aunt Amy lived in the small keeper's quarters. Their three girls spent summers on the island and lived on the mainland with their grandmother during the school year.

I have a vivid memory of visiting the island. The sea was choppy, but I felt safe snuggled against my father's side as Uncle Wes rowed. My cousins were older, and I loved the attention they showered on me. We spent the afternoon gathering periwinkles, then cooking and eating them. (I double-checked this fact with my cousin Mary, because the thought of swallowing periwinkles does not appeal to me now. She assured me they were quite delicious. We will leave it at that.)

Apparently, a colonist who had connections to the river Thames named this small island outside Boothbay Harbor. It seems that England's King John had an affair with a married woman. To soothe her offended husband, the king granted him land along the Thames, and the locals referred to the parcel as "the Cuckold's." (In both old French and English, a cuckold is a man whose wife is unfaithful.)

Boothbay was a busy fishing port during the nineteenth century, and on foggy nights, the Cuckolds posed a formidable threat to approaching ships. President Harrison signed an appropriation in 1892 for a stone fog-signal station and keeper's house. For fifteen years the station sent forth its warning to ships approaching the treacherous shoal, though the sea continually wreaked havoc on the shoddily constructed facility. But there was no accompanying light, so on fogless nights, when no warning sounded, those unfamiliar with the dangers posed by the rocks could still come to grief. A light was needed.

Maine's congressional delegation from Maine used their influence to have a light tower added in 1907. Since the small island could not accommodate additional buildings, the octagonal light tower was built atop the signal house. A two-story keeper's house was added at the same time.

The light was automated in 1975, and the keeper's house was torn down two years after that. Stormy seas continue to break relentlessly around the secluded outpost. The starkness of the ledge and the compact lighthouse tower placidly marking time give little indication of the crucial role this lighthouse has played in the history and development of the surrounding coastal area.

QUILT SQUARE. FOR COLOR PHOTO, SEE P. 19.

This square has a barren, forsaken look, inspired by the actual lighthouse.

Materials Needed

Fabrics:

6½" x 12½" sky piece
3½" x 12½" rocky island piece
4 ocean-color prints, each strip measuring
    1¼" x 12½"
White for house, lower tower, and clouds (or work
    clouds in outline stitch, as in photo)
Gray for granite base
Red for roof
Yellow for light
Black for tower trim and tower top
Black check pattern for door

Black embroidery floss

Assembling the Square

You will first assemble the lighthouse and sky (upper portion of the square), then the ocean waves (lower portion of the square).

1. Prepare pieces for appliqué (p. 7, "How to Appliqué," steps 1–4), referring to the photograph to determine which edges to leave flat because they will be overlapped by other pieces. Patterns for clouds are on p. 103.

2. Pin and baste lighthouse pieces on sky piece, starting with the granite base, positioning its left side about 2½ inches from left edge of sky piece. Next, pin and baste the house in place, fitting its lower edge behind the top of the base. Then do the same with the roof, letting its lower rim overlap the house piece.

3. Once those three pieces are in place, fit the bottom of the tower behind the peak of the roof. Pin and baste.

4. Pin and baste the tower trim, the light, and then the tower top.

5. Using a ¼-inch seam, stitch the rocky island piece to the sky piece.

6. Using the ocean wave guide as a pattern, draw a wavy line across the top of each of the 4 ocean strips. Offset the guide a bit each time so the wave pattern will look more realistic when you assemble the strips. Fold under the top of each strip along these lines. Baste.

7. Assemble the ocean piece. Measure approximately ¾ inch down along the side of ocean strip #1. Align the wavy edge of the next strip on this mark, matching sides. Baste. Next measure down 1¼ inches along the side of strip #2. Align the wavy edge of strip #3 on this mark. Baste. Measure down 1 inch along the side of strip #3 and align the wavy edge of strip #4 on this mark. Baste. Slip-stitch all the strips. The assembled ocean piece should measure 3½ inches on the sides. If it doesn't, cut it to size.

6. Stitch the top edge of the ocean piece to the bottom edge of the rocky island island piece.

7. Appliqué or outline stitch two clouds in the right side of sky.

8. Press.

9. Using 2 strands of floss, add the trim details on house and tower trim and railing around the light(refer to the Cuckolds Light quilt square photograph).

10. Press the finished square.

If the square is to be part of a larger project such as a bedcover or wall hanging, set it aside until you assemble the project.

For a single-square project such as a tote bag or pillow, make a sandwich of completed lighthouse square, batting, and backing. Baste. Complete your project according to the directions in the "Projects, Projects, Projects" chapter.

Quilting Suggestions

Outline quilt around the light tower and along top of ledge and sea. Quilt evenly spaced rows across the granite tower base, using ¼-inch masking tape as a guide. With ¾-inch masking tape to guide you, quilt diagonal lines (p. 11) across the island section. Outline quilt along the top of each ocean strip.

Trace or make photocopy at 100% size. For cloud patterns see p. 103.
Outlines are stitching lines. When cutting, add ⅛" to ¼" outside of lines for seam allowance.
Cut one of each.

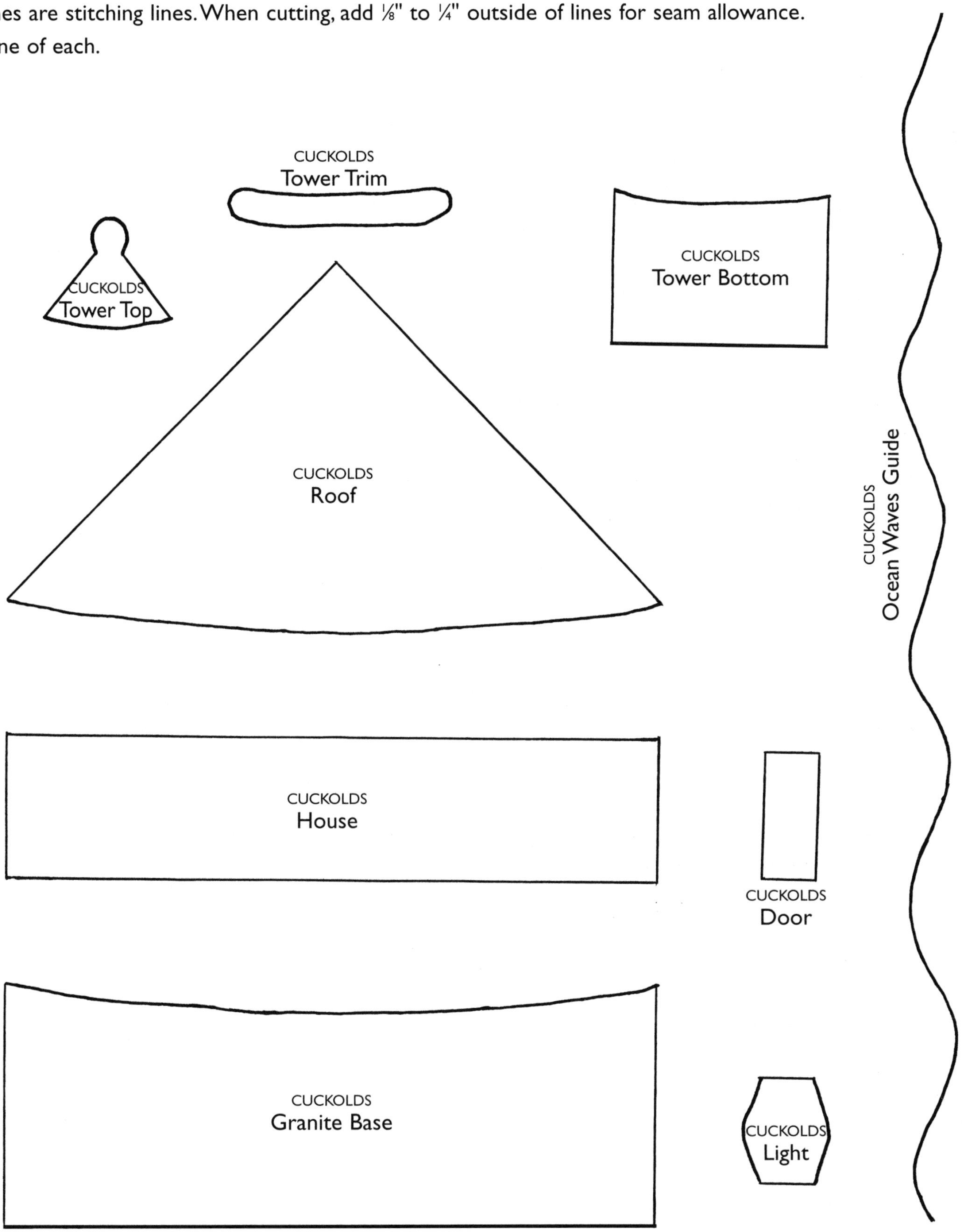

CUCKOLDS
Tower Trim

CUCKOLDS
Tower Top

CUCKOLDS
Tower Bottom

CUCKOLDS
Roof

CUCKOLDS
Ocean Waves Guide

CUCKOLDS
House

CUCKOLDS
Door

CUCKOLDS
Granite Base

CUCKOLDS
Light

Dice Head Light

*E*xplorer Samuel de Champlain discovered the peninsula marking the mouth of the Penobscot and Bagaduce rivers in 1604. He called the area Pentagoet (meaning "falls of the river"). A French trading post was established at the site in 1613. In 1626, Governor Bradford of Massachusetts sent men to this area to establish a trading post for the English commonwealth. The Massachusetts colonists knew the place by the Native American name of Majabagaduce (which probably meant "big tidal salt bay." Nine years later, in 1635, the French regained control and held it until 1651.

The ensuing years found the region in a state of political disarray. In 1667, a treaty deeded the whole of Acadia, including Pentagoet, to the French. Around the same time, Jean-Vincent de l'Abbadie de St. Castin was discharged from the French army and obtained a grant for the land, which now bears his name—Castine. He befriended the Wabanaki Indians, and the next sixty years were tranquil at his trading post.

In 1759, the British realized the value of the area, and arrived with an army to establish Fort George. The Union Jack was hoisted, and by the onset of the Revolution, families were moving into the village to establish businesses. The colonists heard about the English occupation and sent twenty-four ships and fourteen hundred ill-prepared militiamen to take the fort, leading to the worst naval defeat in American history. The Americans misjudged the strength of those commanding the fort. Twice, Commodore Saltonstall engaged the three British men-of-war anchored across the entrance to the harbor, with little damage suffered by either side. The attempt at landing and engaging ground troops was partially successful but never completed, allowing the last attempt to be thwarted by an eighteen-year-old English lieutenant.

The American fleet procrastinated, dropping anchor at the mouth of the Penobscot River long enough for British naval vessels to arrive from Halifax. The superior English force chased the Americans up the Penobscot River, where they were forced to scuttle their ships. Despite this Loyalist victory, Castine became part of the new country when the war ended and the boundary between the United States and Canada was set at the St. Croix River. The British captured the fort again during the War of 1812, and Castine remained under British rule until the end of that war.

Due to its strategic location, Castine played a major role in world maritime trade during the prosperous days of shipping. Dice Head Light was built in 1828 to provide safe passage at Castine and along the Penobscot River. Built of rubblestone, the original tower was surrounded by a hexagonal wooden frame that was removed during the late 1800s, leaving only the cone-shaped tower.

This lovely square is attractive either alone or combined with other squares in a larger project. Flanked by two plain quilting squares with sashing strips and a border, this design makes a great table runner.

Part of this quilt square's appeal is the integration of the various green shades of the trees and shrubs. Place lighter shades in back and darker shades in the foreground. Add texture by incorporating a mix of prints.

Materials Needed

Fabrics:

8½" x 12½" piece for sky background

4½" x 12½" piece for grass (green print)

Brown for road

White for tower, shed, cupola, and clouds (or work clouds in outline stitch, if you prefer)

Black for tower section and tower top

Light red for outbuilding

Dark red for outbuilding side section

Dark gray for outbuilding roof

Light gray for cupola and shed roofs

9 different green prints for trees and shrubs—

1 light, 2 medium, 2 dark for shrubs, 4 prints for triangle trees

Yellow for light

Black embroidery floss

Assembling the Square

1. Prepare pieces for appliqué (p. 7, "How to Appliqué," steps 1–4), referring to the photograph to determine which edges to leave flat because they will be overlapped by other pieces.

2. Baste road piece to grass piece. Slip-stitch in place.

3. Pin triangle trees to sky piece: trees A, 1st B, and C are at center; 2nd tree B is on right of tower.

4. Pin middle shrub, back shrub, 4 tower pieces, 2 shed pieces, and 6 outbuilding and cupola pieces to the sky piece.

5. Baste all pinned pieces in place, rearranging as necessary; slip-stitch.

6. Pin and baste left shrub to front of outbuilding and right shrub to tower; slip-stitch.

7. Now, stitch grass section to sky section, using a ¼-inch seam allowance.

8. If using appliqué clouds, pin, baste, and stitch them into place. (Cloud patterns are on p. 103.)

9. Press.

10. Using 2 strands of floss, add the trim details on tower trim and light (refer to the Dice Head Light quilt square photograph).

11. Press the finished square.

If the square is to be part of a larger project such as a bedcover or wall hanging, set it aside until you assemble the project.

For a single-square project such as a tote bag or pillow, make a sandwich of completed lighthouse square, batting, and backing. Baste. Complete your project according to the directions in the "Projects, Projects, Projects" chapter.

QUILT SQUARE. FOR COLOR PHOTO, SEE P. 19.

Quilting Suggestions

Outline quilt trees, shrubs, buildings, tower, and road. Quilt shingle rows on outbuilding roof, using masking tape. Quilt branches on large shrubs, using designs from "Smaller Quilting Patterns" (pps. 109–111). Quilt random lines on road to represent ruts. Using tree quilting designs (page 111), quilt two to three trees on left side of square.

Trace or make photocopy at 100% size. Cut one of each unless otherwise noted.

Solid lines are stitching lines. When cutting, add ⅛" to ¼" outside of lines for seam allowance. Dashed lines are cutting lines for edges that will align with edge of quilt square.

For cloud patterns see p. 103.

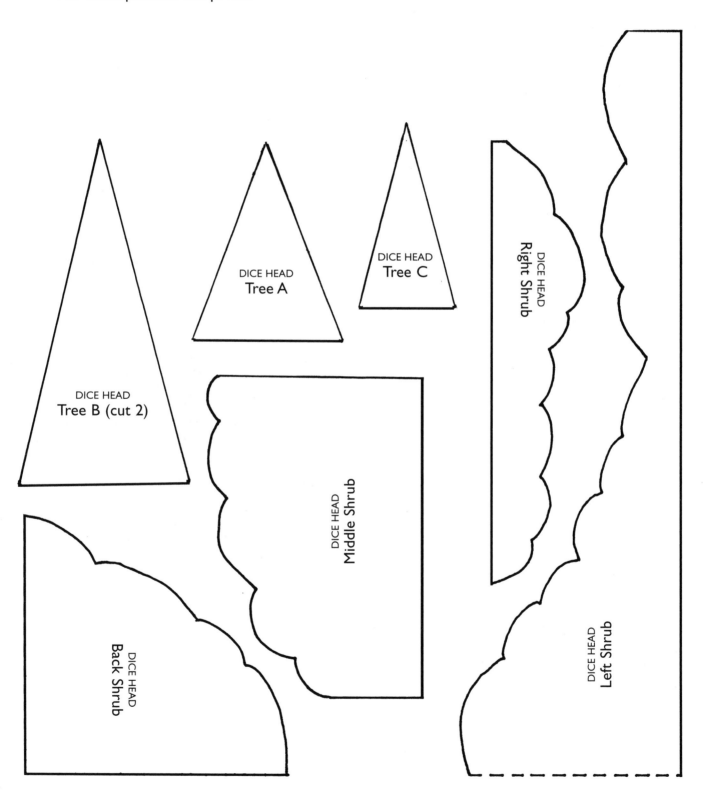

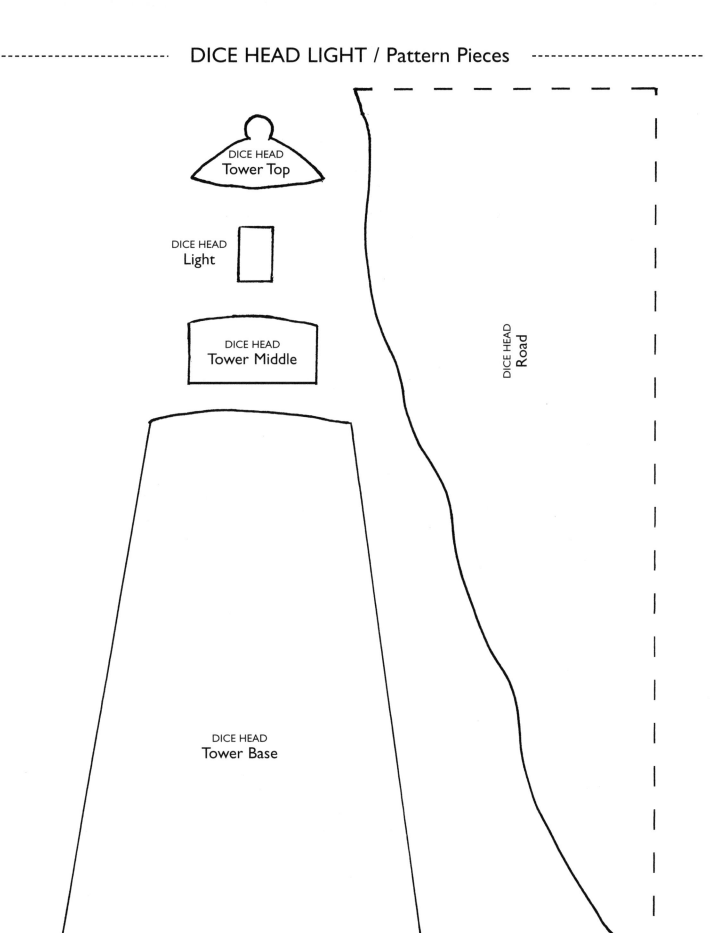

DICE HEAD
Tower Top

DICE HEAD
Light

DICE HEAD
Tower Middle

DICE HEAD
Tower Base

DICE HEAD
Road

Trace or make photocopy at 100% size. Cut one of each.

Solid lines are stitching lines. When cutting, add ⅛" to ¼" outside of lines for seam allowance.

Dashed lines are cutting lines for edges that will align with edge of quilt square.

For cloud patterns see p. 103.

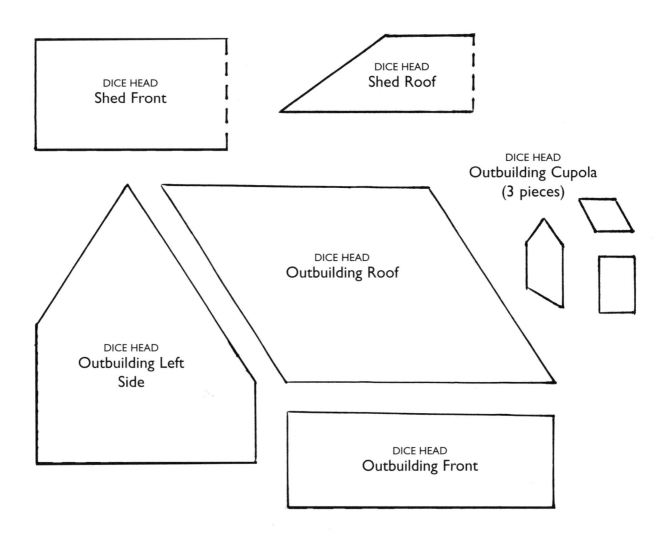

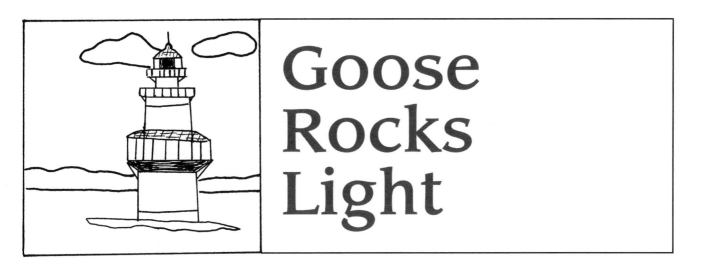

Goose Rocks Light

*G*oose Rocks Light stands alone, surrounded by the sea. It guards the eastern end of the Fox Islands Thorofare, the narrow waterway separating North Haven and Vinalhaven islands. In 1603, Captain Martin Pring of Bristol, England, anchored his sailing vessels Speedwell *and* Discoverer *in this passageway. Pring and his men were so struck by the beauty of the wooded islands, and the proliferation of gray foxes inhabiting them, that he called them the Fox Islands. They were known by this name until 1790.*

Built on a concrete caisson, this open-water light resembles a huge spark plug setting on its ledge base. The circular tower was constructed in 1890 from prefabricated cast iron, chosen in lieu of Vinalhaven granite to reduce construction costs. For seventy-three years, the keepers of Goose Rocks lived inside the fifty-one-foot tower. The three-story bachelor station contained cramped living quarters, with only the narrow walkway around the outside offering a breath of fresh sea air.

Goose Rocks Light is red, with a white sector, and flashes every six seconds. Its fourth-order Fresnel lens allows the red sector to be seen for eleven miles and the white sector for twelve miles.

*T*his tower, with its rusty foundation, has an appeal all its own. Once you complete the square, imagine standing at the walkway railing on a perfect Maine summer's day, with the salty air blowing against your skin. That's my idea of heaven.

Materials Needed

Fabrics:

8½" x 12½" sky piece

4½" x 12½" sea piece

Green for island pieces

Dark brown for ledge

Rust shade for tower section 1 (base)

Second rust shade for lower tower trim (optional)

White for tower sections 2, 3, and 4, and clouds

Red check for tower light

Pale print for tower top and mid-tower trim

Rust and black embroidery floss for trim on tower and base

Assembling the Square

You will first assemble the background square, then add the lighthouse and clouds.

1. Prepare pieces for appliqué (p. 7, "How to Appliqué," steps 1–4), referring to the photograph to determine which edges to leave flat because they will be overlapped by other pieces.

2. Fold under and baste the top edge of each land piece. Match bottoms and sides of the island and sky pieces and baste across.

3. Using a ¼-inch seam, stitch the sea piece to bottom of the island pieces, making a background square.

4. Cut two clouds. Baste into place. (Cloud patterns are on p. 103).

5. Pin the lighthouse pieces to the background square. Fit one cloud slightly behind left side of tower. Pin second cloud to right of tower. Pin ledge at bottom of tower. When the placement is satisfactory, baste and slip-stitch the pieces in place.

6. Press.

7. Referring to picture and using two strands of rust embroidery floss, embroider tower trim. With two strands of black floss, embroider a horizontal line near the bottom of the tower base.

If the square is to be part of a larger project such as a bedcover or wall hanging, set it aside until you assemble the project.

For a single-square project such as a tote bag or pillow, make a sandwich of completed lighthouse square, batting, and backing. Baste.

Complete your project according to the directions in the "Projects, Projects, Projects" chapter.

Quilting Suggestion

Outline quilt around each piece. Quilt waves on the sea piece.

QUILT SQUARE. FOR COLOR PHOTOGRAPH, SEE P. 20.

GOOSE ROCKS LIGHT / Pattern Pieces

Trace or make photocopy at 100% size. Cut one of each. For cloud patterns see p. 103.
Solid lines are stitching lines. When cutting, add ⅛" to ¼" outside of lines for seam allowance.
Dashed lines are cutting lines.

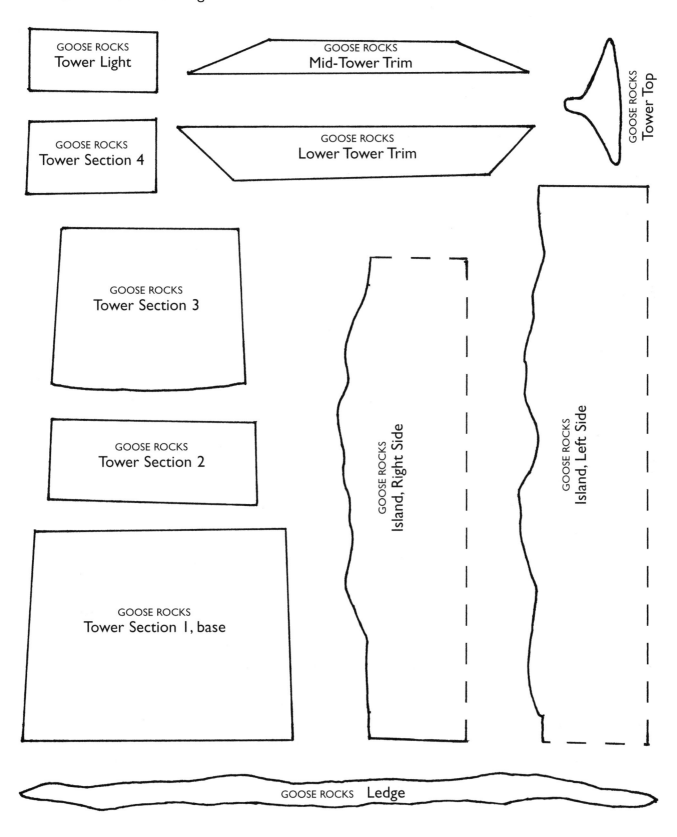

Grindle Point Light

I *slesboro is one of the more famous of the two thousand islands dotting Maine's coast. Situated in Penobscot Bay, this narrow, ten-mile strip of land has long been home to men who garner their living from its waters. Long before land-lubbers discovered its beautiful shoreline, whaling crews and fishermen made use of its significant location.*

The island measures just a few yards at its narrowest point, and up to three miles at its widest. The first permanent settlers dropped anchor here in 1760. While the island has in the past been known as Long, One-Hundred-Acre, Lime, Marshal, and Lasell Island, it is now simply referred to as Islesboro, although the incorporated town of Islesboro includes more than the one large island.

Grindle Point Light stands at the north side of Gilkey Harbor on land originally owned by Francis Grindel, who became the second keeper of the light.

The weather took its toll on the original twenty-eight-foot structure, built in 1850. In 1874, it was replaced by the thirty-nine-foot, square brick tower still standing watch over the harbor entrance today.

In 1934, the lighthouse was decommissioned when keeper William Dodge retired. A skeleton tower was erected to take its place. The local population campaigned to have the original light preserved as a monument to seafaring island men. In 1987, the skeleton tower was removed and a solar optic replaced the fifth-order Fresnel lens in in the old tower. Once again, the green light at Grindle Point, flashing every four seconds, can be seen from the mainland. The lighthouse is located near the ferry landing and is now a museum.

T his simple square would look nice as the center piece of a wall hanging.

Materials Needed

Fabrics:

    8" x 12½" sky piece
    5" x 12½" sea piece
    Tan for rocky ground
    Green for hills
    White for tower, shed, and cloud
    Dark gray for shed roof
    Black for tower top, trim pieces, and windows
    Black check for shed windows
    Light green check for tower light
    Dark green for shrub

Black embroidery floss for tower trim

Assembling the Square

You will assemble the background (upper portion of square), then attach foreground land and sea before adding the appliqué pieces.

1. Prepare pieces for appliqué (p. 7, "How to Appliqué," steps 1–4), referring to the photograph to determine which edges to leave flat because they will be overlapped by other pieces.

2. Fold under and baste top seam of hills piece. Matching bottoms, baste hills to sky piece. Slip-stitch hills in place.

QUILT SQUARE. FOR COLOR PHOTOGRAPH, SEE P. 21.

3. Fold under top seam of rocky ground. Matching sides and bottoms, baste to sea piece. Slip-stitch across top of rocky ground piece.

4. Stitch sea and sky together using a ¼-inch seam, forming background square.

5. Pin and baste shed, shed roof, and tower to background square; slip-stitch.

6. Next, appliqué the tower trims, tower light, and windows on tower and shed.

7. Using the Grindle Point quilt square photo as a guide, appliqué the shrub to front of tower, and a cloud in the sky. Press.

8. Using 2 strands of floss, add the trim details on tower trim and light (refer to the Grindle Point Light quilt square photograph).

9. Press the finished square.

If the square is to be part of a larger project such as a bedcover or wall hanging, set it aside until you assemble the project.

For a single-square project such as a tote bag or pillow, make a sandwich of completed lighthouse square, batting, and backing. Baste.

Complete your project according to the directions in the "Projects, Projects, Projects" chapter.

Quilting Suggestions

Outline quilt around rocky ground, tower, and shed. Quilt waves on sea and random lines on rocky ground.

Quilt panes on shed window and branches on shrub. Wave and branches quilting patterns can be found on pages 102 and 111.

Trace or make photocopy at 100% size. Cut one of each. For cloud patterns see p. 103.

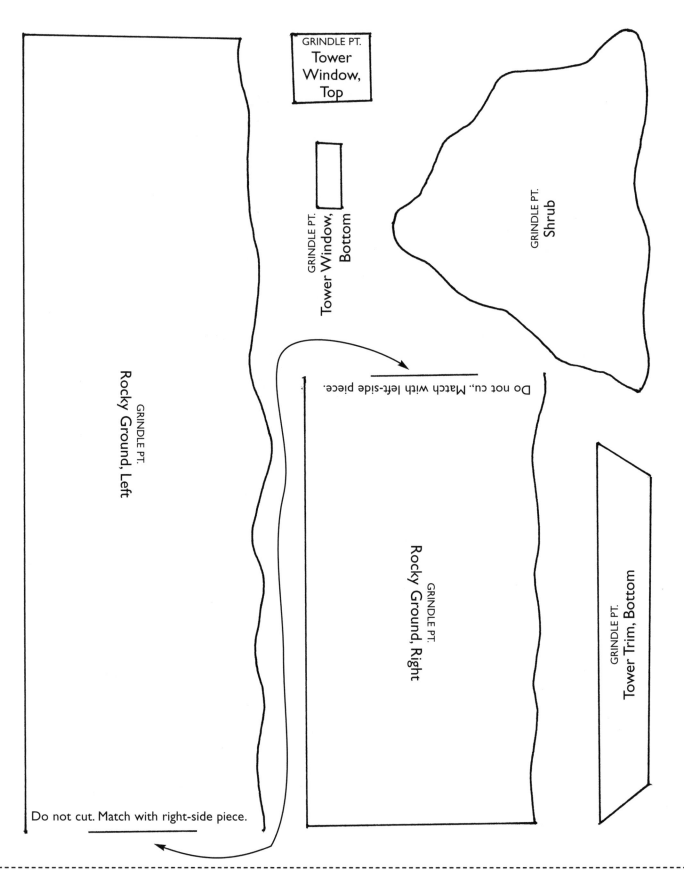

GRINDLE PT.
Tower Window, Top

GRINDLE PT.
Tower Window, Bottom

GRINDLE PT.
Shrub

GRINDLE PT.
Rocky Ground, Left

Do not cut. Match with left-side piece.

GRINDLE PT.
Rocky Ground, Right

GRINDLE PT.
Tower Trim, Bottom

Do not cut. Match with right-side piece.

Solid lines are stitching lines. When cutting, add ⅛" to ¼" outside of lines for seam allowance.
Dashed lines are cutting lines for edges that will align with edge of quilt square.

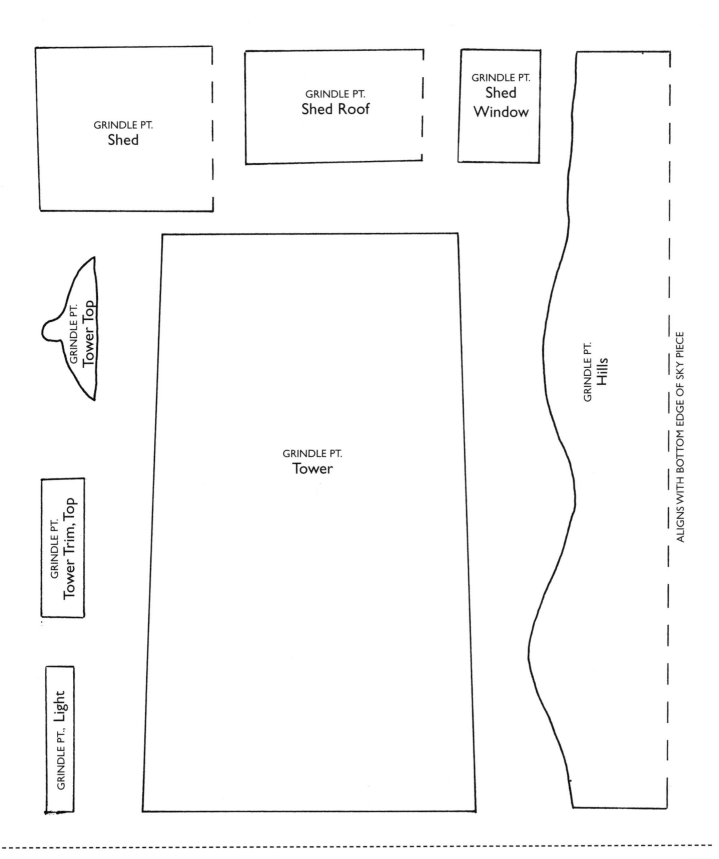

GRINDLE PT.
Shed

GRINDLE PT.
Shed Roof

GRINDLE PT.
Shed
Window

GRINDLE PT.
Tower Top

GRINDLE PT.
Tower Trim, Top

GRINDLE PT., Light

GRINDLE PT.
Tower

GRINDLE PT.
Hills

ALIGNS WITH BOTTOM EDGE OF SKY PIECE

Kennebec River Range Lights

*T*he Kennebec River was an important waterway long before the birth of this country. Sailing vessels made their way through its hazardous currents without land navigational aids. Today, several lighthouses efficiently placed along the riverbanks aid ships traversing to and from the open sea.

Built in 1898, the Kennebec River Range Lights are the only range lights in Maine. Because of their precise placement, a river pilot knows his vessel is safely in the deep river channel when he sees these lights in the correct alignment.

Each tower is equipped with a white fifth-order Fresnel lens. The front light continually blinks a quick flash. The rear light beams six quick flashes followed by a pause. The front tower stands thirty-three feet above mean high water level, and the rear tower stands at eighteen feet. The towers are exactly 235 yards apart.

Karen McLean, bosun's mate, U.S. Coast Guard, was the last keeper of the Kennebec River Range Lights. This was one of the country's last light stations to be automated, in 1990.

An oft-told story connected to this part of the Maine coast has a smidgen of miracle attached to it. The tale is often set at the Kennebec River Range Lights, though some accounts place the events at Hendricks Head Light, which lies at the mouth of Sheepscot River. Did these events really occur, or is this a taradiddle?* You decide:

One stormy March night in the 1870s, the lightkeeper sighted a ship foundering on a ledge. The ship began breaking apart as the people on board scrambled into the frozen rigging. It was impossible for the keeper to attempt a rescue by himself, but he built a large fire to alert the ship's crew that they had been spotted.

The keeper continued to feed the fire as the outlook became more and more desperate. Suddenly he noticed a large, wave-tossed object blowing in to shore. The waterlogged bundle turned out to be two feather mattresses tied together. Ripping them apart, he discovered a box with a baby tucked inside, screaming loudly. Pinned to the tiny girl's blanket were a locket and a handwritten note commending the child's fate to God.

The keeper knew he should let the shipwrecked passengers know he had found the child, but when he looked back out to the wave-swept ledge, he saw that the ship had completely disappeared. There was no one left to signal.

* Taradiddle: a story recounted so often that it is taken as the truth

QUILT SQUARE. FOR COLOR PHOTOGRAPH, SEE P. 22.

Both Range Light towers sit back from the riverbank. This square shows each tower distinctly. The perspective is correct, although the walkway to the front tower is not represented, to allow for easier execution of the patch.

It is amazing that these quaint wooden towers sitting in a grassy meadow have played such a vital role in ensuring the safe passage of countless ships.

Fabrics Needed

9½" x 12½" sky piece
3½" x 12½" grass piece
10 different greens for trees (light for farthest trees, medium in the middle, darkest in foreground)
White for towers
Red for tower roofs
Small black or gray check for tower windows
Gray for back tower base

Assembling the Square

1. Prepare pieces for appliqué (see p. 7, steps 1–4).

2. Pin trees to sky material. Baste, then slip-stitch trees in place.

3. Baste towers, back tower base, and windows in place. Slip-stitch to background.

4. Stitch grass piece to sky piece using ¼-inch seam.

5. Press.

If the square is to be part of a larger project such as a bedcover or wall hanging, set it aside until you assemble the project.

For a single-square project such as a tote bag or pillow, make a sandwich of completed lighthouse square, batting, and backing. Baste.

Complete your project according to the directions in the "Projects, Projects, Projects" chapter.

Quilting Suggestions

Draw branches on each tree. This can be done freehand, or you can use the branches patterns provided on page 110. Quilt these.

Outline quilt around towers, tower roofs, and windows. Quilt lines marked on towers and tower roofs.

Using ¾-inch masking tape, quilt diagonal gridlines across the grass (p. 11).

Trace or make photocopy at
100% size. Cut one of each.

Solid lines are stitching
lines. When cutting, add
⅛" to ¼" outside of lines
for seam allowance.

Dashed lines are cutting
lines for edges that will
align with edge of quilt
square.

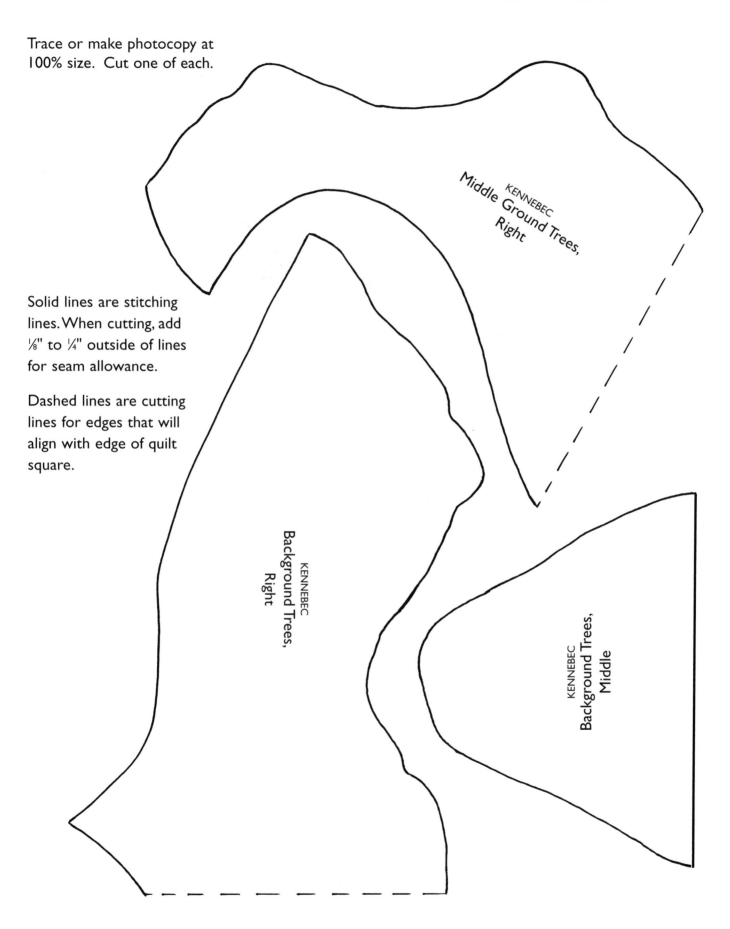

KENNEBEC
Middle Ground Trees,
Right

KENNEBEC
Background Trees,
Right

KENNEBEC
Background Trees,
Middle

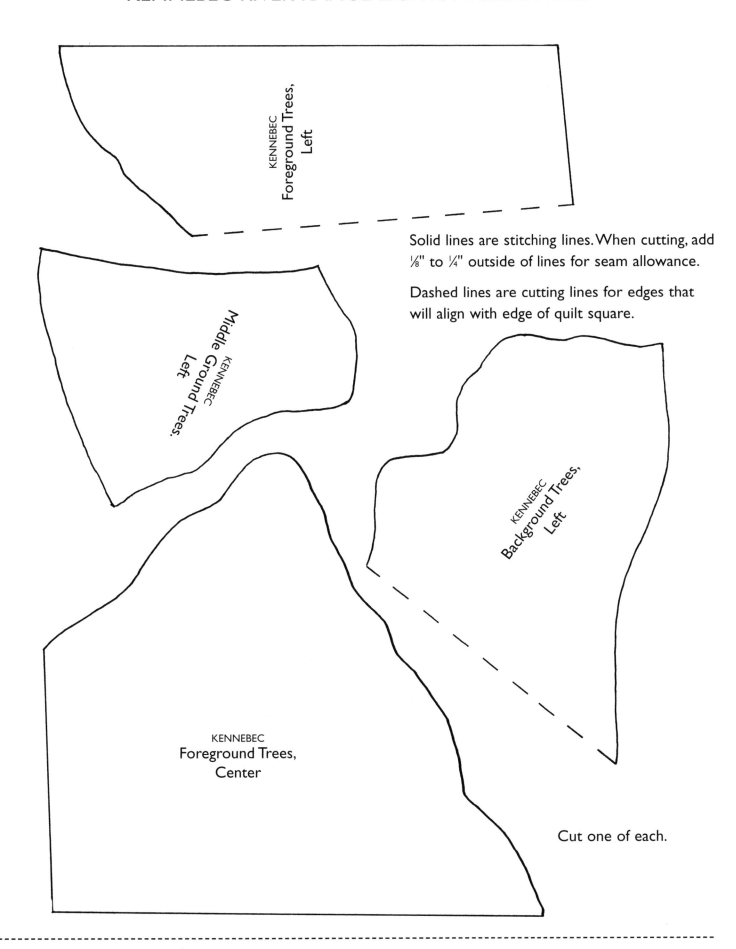

KENNEBEC
Foreground Trees,
Left

Solid lines are stitching lines. When cutting, add ⅛" to ¼" outside of lines for seam allowance.

Dashed lines are cutting lines for edges that will align with edge of quilt square.

Middle
Ground Trees,
Left
KENNEBEC

KENNEBEC
Background Trees,
Left

KENNEBEC
Foreground Trees,
Center

Cut one of each.

Trace or make photocopy at 100% size.
Cut one of each.

Solid outlines are
stitching lines.
When cutting, add
⅛" to ¼" outside
of lines for seam
allowance.

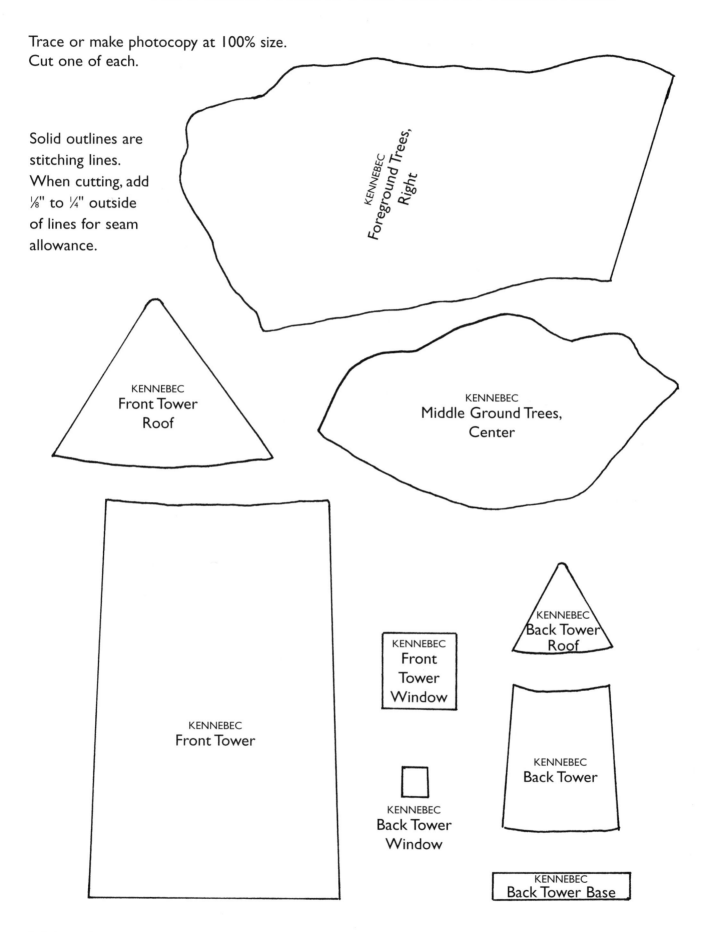

KENNEBEC
Foreground Trees,
Right

KENNEBEC
Front Tower
Roof

KENNEBEC
Middle Ground Trees,
Center

KENNEBEC
Front Tower

KENNEBEC
Front
Tower
Window

KENNEBEC
Back Tower
Window

KENNEBEC
Back Tower
Roof

KENNEBEC
Back Tower

KENNEBEC
Back Tower Base

Marshall Point Light

*T*his beautiful lighthouse is my favorite because it has always been part of my life. I grew up in Port Clyde and know Marshall Point from both land and sea. Although I never truly appreciated the town and its lighthouse until I left, my parents were friends with several light keepers there, and I have eaten many dinners in the keeper's dining room.

The original 1832 keeper's house burned down after a lightning strike in 1895 and was replaced with the present gambrel-roofed dwelling. Duty at Marshall Point was a coveted position, since the danger at this mainland light station was minimal—unless you were in a vessel during a storm.

I remember the morning in 1954 when the town was abuzz with tragic news: A sailboat out of Boothbay Harbor had washed onto the rocks near the lighthouse. The 35-foot sloop Truant was a victim of hurricane Carol. The couple aboard were valiantly trying to reach the harbor at Port Clyde when the force of violent winds and tumultuous waves smashed their rudder. As they were being pushed about by the maelstrom, the husband, frantically trying to make repairs, was washed over the side. He was not wearing a life jacket.

The woman was suddenly alone as the ocean spewed over the gunwales. Realizing that Truant was going to crash onto the rocks, she donned a life jacket and jumped into the boiling sea. Pitched and tossed by the waves, she eventually washed ashore at Hupper's Island, on the opposite side of the harbor, and was rescued from there.

The spot where the sailboat went onto the ledges was only a few hundred feet from the harbor entrance. Not far on a calm day, but for people in a rudderless boat, battling winds and raging waters, it was like trying to cross the Atlantic. There was no human control over the situation. The stalwart lighthouse tower was no help to people in a crippled vessel.

Marshall Point Light's original soapstone tower was completely redone in 1858. The new thirty-one-foot tower, built on a rock outcropping, was connected to land by a wooden walkway supported by granite columns. The tower base was also built of granite blocks, and bricks completed the upper section. It was equipped with a fifth-order Fresnel lens, casting a beam that reached twelve miles.

The tower still guards the entrance to Port Clyde harbor, once known as Herring Gut. The St. George Historical Society now maintains a museum in the ell of the keeper's residence.

QUILT SQUARE. FOR COLOR PHOTOGRAPH, SEE P. 22.

There are countless depictions of Marshall Point Light, each with its own appeal. This view offers a general view of the light and its surroundings. The square is an exercise in patience, but the end result will bring extreme satisfaction.

Materials Needed

Fabrics:
  3½" x 12½" sky piece
  9½" x 12½" sea piece
  White for granite columns
  White prints for tower base, rails, and supports
  Gray or brown for rocky ground piece
  Green for grass
  2 other greens for islands
  Gray for walkway
  Black for tower midsection, top, and trim
  Light blue or silver for door
  Yellow for light
Black embroidery floss for trim

Assembling the Square

You will first assemble the background, then put all the walkway and tower pieces in place, working generally from left to right.

1. Prepare pieces for appliqué (p. 7, "How to Appliqué," steps 1–4), referring to the photograph to determine which edges to leave flat because they will be overlapped by other pieces.

2. Using a ¼-inch seam allowance, stitch sky to sea.

3. Baste islands in place. Slip-stitch to background.

4. Pin and baste rocky ground and grass to background square; slip-stitch.

5. Pin all remaining pieces to background, correcting placement, before doing any basting. (The following measurements are approximate; some manipulating will be required in this fairly complicated layout, and your end result may not be exactly like the photograph, but as long as the view is the same, it will be all right.) Working from left to right, place bottom edge of front support piece ¾ inch from the bottom of square. Match sides. Place mid-support piece ½ inch above right side of front support, and back support piece ⅞ inch above right side of mid-support.

6. Fit bottom of granite tower base 1⅜ inches above the back support.

7. Finish placing tower pieces to the top of tower base. Pin door in place.

8. Fitting the walkway parts is not hard, but it is time consuming. Start by pinning bottom rail in place, then place walkway, and finally, the mid-rail.

9. Referring to picture, pin front-row rail supports in place, starting with #6. Then, position and pin the back row of supports. Place and pin top rail. Some manipulating of these pieces may be necessary.

10. When placement is satisfactory, baste all pieces; finally, slip-stitch. Press.

11. Using 2 strands of floss, add the trim details on tower trim and light (refer to the Marshall Point Light quilt square photograph).

12. Press the finished square.

If the square is to be part of a larger project such as a bedcover or wall hanging, set it aside until you assemble the project.

For a single-square project such as a tote bag or pillow, make a sandwich of completed lighthouse square, batting, and backing. Baste.

Complete your project according to the directions in the "Projects, Projects, Projects" chapter.

Quilting Suggestions

Outline quilt around each piece. Using ¾-inch masking tape, quilt granite blocks on walkway supports and tower granite base. Quilt diagonal lines (p. 11) on the rocky ground and grass section. Quilt waves on the sea.

Trace or make photocopy at 100% size. Cut one of each.
Solid lines are stitching lines. When cutting, add ⅛" to ¼" outside of lines for seam allowance.
Dashed lines are cutting lines for edges that will align with edge of quilt square.

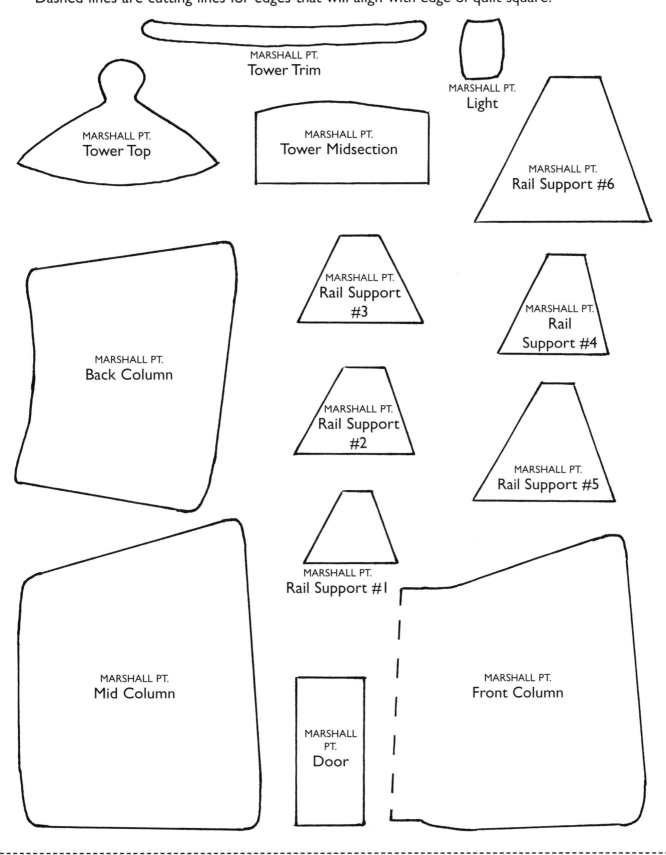

MARSHALL PT.
Tower Trim

MARSHALL PT.
Light

MARSHALL PT.
Tower Top

MARSHALL PT.
Tower Midsection

MARSHALL PT.
Rail Support #6

MARSHALL PT.
Rail Support
#3

MARSHALL PT.
Rail
Support #4

MARSHALL PT.
Back Column

MARSHALL PT.
Rail Support
#2

MARSHALL PT.
Rail Support #5

MARSHALL PT.
Rail Support #1

MARSHALL PT.
Mid Column

MARSHALL
PT.
Door

MARSHALL PT.
Front Column

Solid lines are stitching lines. When cutting, add ⅛" to ¼" outside of lines for seam allowance.
Dashed lines are cutting lines for edges that will align with edge of quilt square.

Trace or make photo-copy at 100% size. Cut one of each.

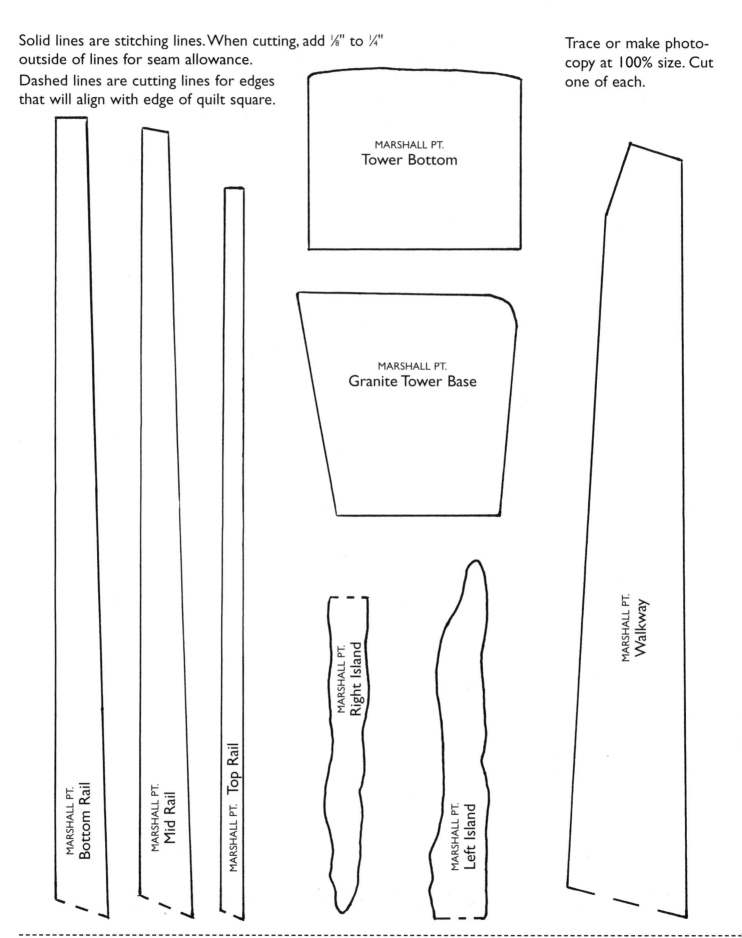

MARSHALL PT.
Tower Bottom

MARSHALL PT.
Granite Tower Base

MARSHALL PT.
Bottom Rail

MARSHALL PT.
Mid Rail

MARSHALL PT.
Top Rail

MARSHALL PT.
Right Island

MARSHALL PT.
Left Island

MARSHALL PT.
Walkway

Trace or make photocopy at 100% size. Cut one of each.

Solid lines are stitching lines. When cutting, add ⅛" to ¼" outside of lines for seam allowance.

Dashed lines are cutting lines for edges that will align with edge of quilt square.

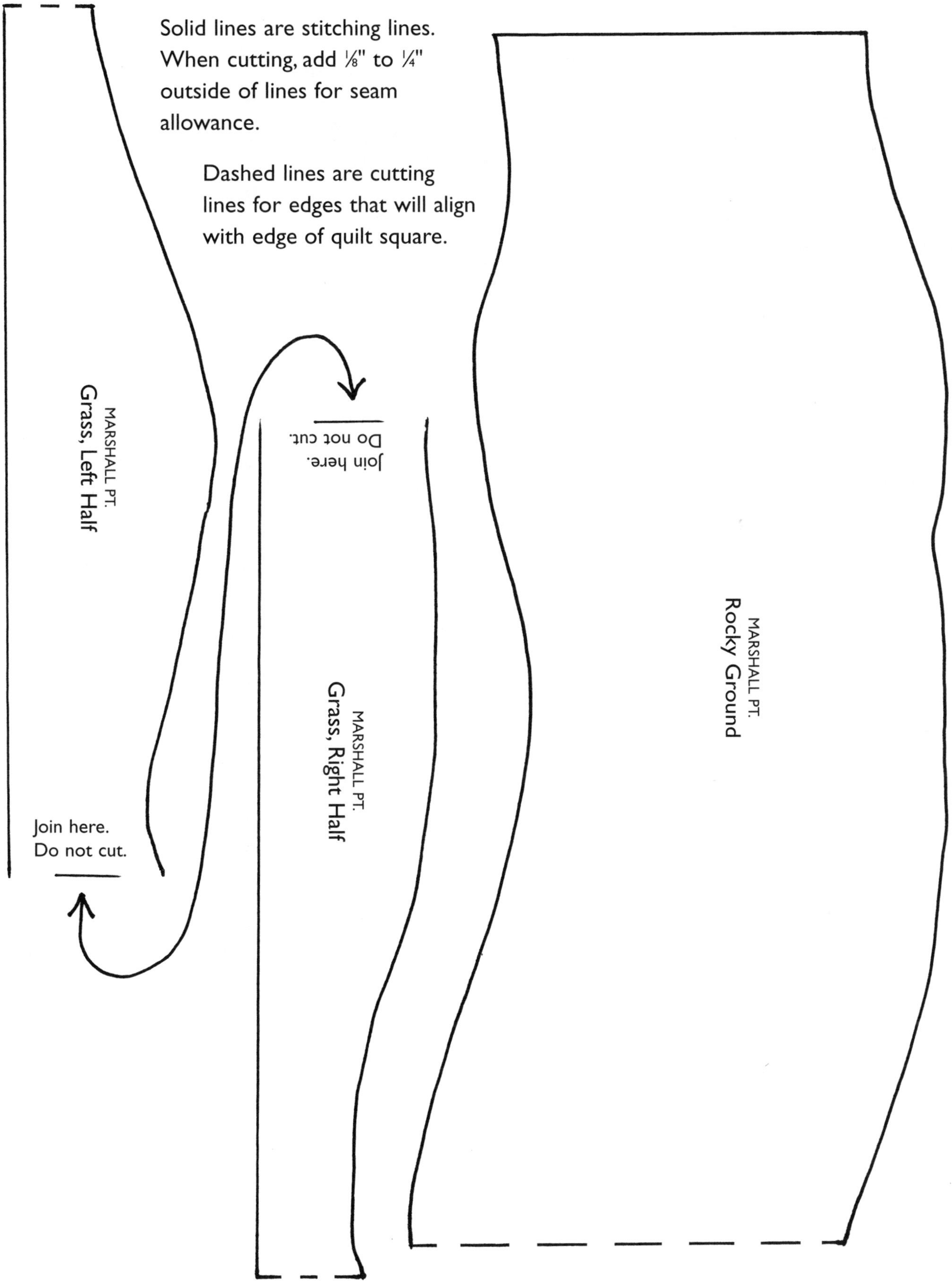

MARSHALL PT.
Grass, Left Half

Join here.
Do not cut.

Join here.
Do not cut.

MARSHALL PT.
Grass, Right Half

MARSHALL PT.
Rocky Ground

Monhegan Island Light

*T*he sheer, rugged cliffs of Monhegan Island rise from the ocean ten miles off the mainland. Captain John Smith called this place Barties, Indian for "the island," originally a prime fishing ground for them. For centuries, European fishermen knew of the outermost Maine islands and the rich fishing grounds that lay offshore of them. Puritans from the Massachusetts Bay Colony also visited the island.

French Baron Jean-Vincent d'Abbadie de St. Castin came from Castine to attack both Monhegan and Pemaquid and lay claim to the land for the French Crown. With help from the Indians, Castin succeeded in destroying the Pemaquid settlement in 1689.

Monhegan was later owned by the Davidson family of Boston. They finally grew tired of the raids and sold it in 1749 to tinsmith Shem Drowne, the artist who created the famous grasshopper weathervane that still graces Boston's Faneuil Hall. Drowne purchased Monhegan's 440 acres for ten pounds, thirteen shillings. In 1770, Shem's son sold the island for a handsome profit.

On September 5, 1813, the British brig Boxer and the American square-rigger Enterprise clashed in the waters between Port Clyde and Monhegan. The Americans emerged victorious, and the rest, as they say, is history. During this thirty-five-minute battle, both captains met their demise and were buried side by side in Portland.

A lighthouse was essential at this location, since Monhegan was often the first land sighted by ships arriving from the east. it was built on the island's highest point, and the first beam shone from Monhegan Island Light on July 2, 1824. This original structure was replaced by a forty-eight-foot granite tower that stood 178 feet above the sea. Its beacon consisted of ten lamps with sixteen-inch reflectors, which produced a red-and-white flash visible for twenty miles. Both sperm oil and lard oil were used to keep the lamps shining. The multiple lamps and reflectors were replaced by a second-order Fresnel lens in 1856.

In 1861, John Humphrey was charged with tending the Monhegan Light. When he died nine months later, his widow, Betty, became the light keeper and held the post from 1862 until 1880. Her son, Edward came home to help his mother with the operation of the lighthouse after he was disabled in the Civil War,.

The light was automated in 1959. The keeper's house still stands, thanks to the island's year-round and summer residents, who voted overwhelmingly to make it into an island museum.

This patch depicts the boathouse, a small shed, and the tower. The boat is a perfect example of a light keeper's transportation a century or more ago. This square takes a little more time to finish than do some of the others, although it is a simple pattern. I only wish it were as easy to incorporate the island's six hundred varieties of wildflowers and two hundred species of birds into a quilt patch!

Materials Needed

Fabrics:

8" x 12½" sky piece

5" x 12½" grass piece

Gray print for tower

White for boat house (and optional cloud)

Red for boat house roof, boat bottom, tower top, and side of small shed

Darker red for gable end of small shed

Dark gray for shed roof, tower trim, and windows

Red or neutral color check for tower light section

Light gray for boat body

Salmon shade for boat interior

Green for bush

Striped fabric for boat house ramp

Off-white for boat house door

Black embroidery floss for tower trim

Assembling the Square

1. Prepare pieces for appliqué (p. 7, "How to Appliqué," steps 1–4), referring to the photograph to determine which edges to leave flat because they will be overlapped by other pieces. Patterns for clouds can be found on p. 103.

2. Using a ¼-inch seam allowance, stitch the sky piece to the grass piece.

3. Position the tree and tower pieces to background. Baste in place.

4. Next, position and pin the small shed and roof to background. Baste.

5. Repeat step #4 with the boat house side, front, and roof pieces.

6. Slip-stitch the basted pieces to the background.

7. Baste boat, door, ramp, and windows in place (and clouds, if using). Slip-stitch these pieces. Press.

8. Using 2 strands of floss, add the trim details on tower trim (refer to the Monhegan Island Light quilt square photograph).

9. Press the finished square.

If the square is to be part of a larger project such as a bedcover or wall hanging, set it aside until you assemble the project.

For a single-square project such as a tote bag or pillow, make a sandwich of completed lighthouse square, batting, and backing. Baste. Complete your project according to the directions in the "Projects, Projects, Projects" chapter.

Quilting Suggestions

Outline quilt around each piece. Using ¼-inch masking tape as a guide, quilt rows to represent shingles on boathouse roof. Using the tree quilting designs on page 111, quilt two trees on the lower right side.

QUILT SQUARE. FOR COLOR PHOTOGRAPH, SEE P. 23.

Solid lines are stitching lines. When cutting, add ⅛"
to ¼" outside of lines for seam allowance.

Dashed lines are cutting lines for edges that
will align with edge of quilt square.

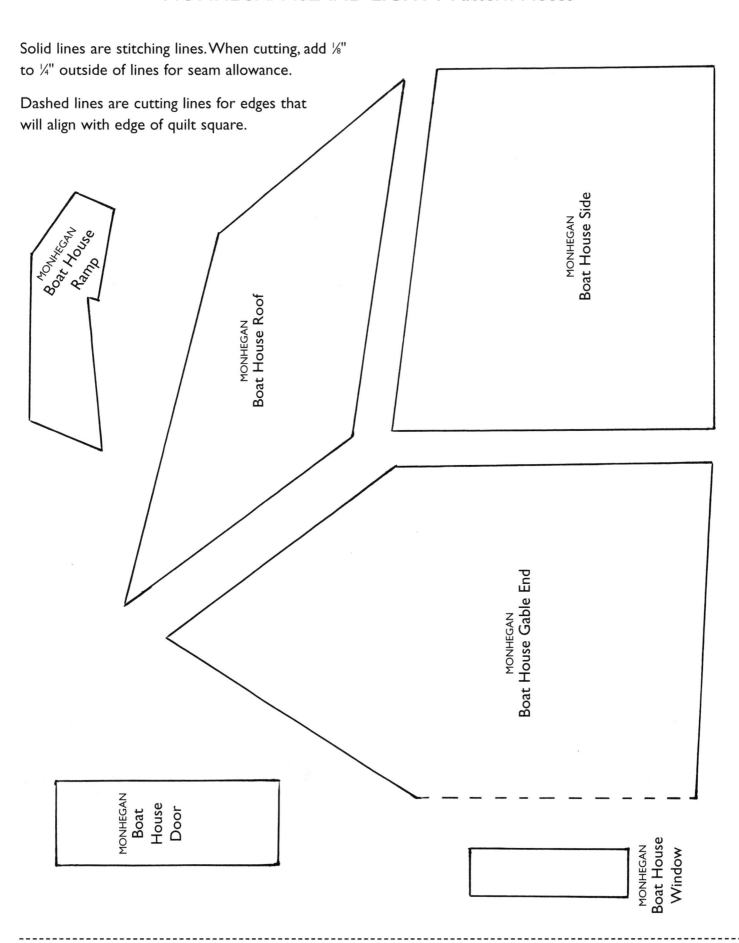

MONHEGAN
Boat House Ramp

MONHEGAN
Boat House Roof

MONHEGAN
Boat House Side

MONHEGAN
Boat House Gable End

MONHEGAN
Boat House Door

MONHEGAN
Boat House Window

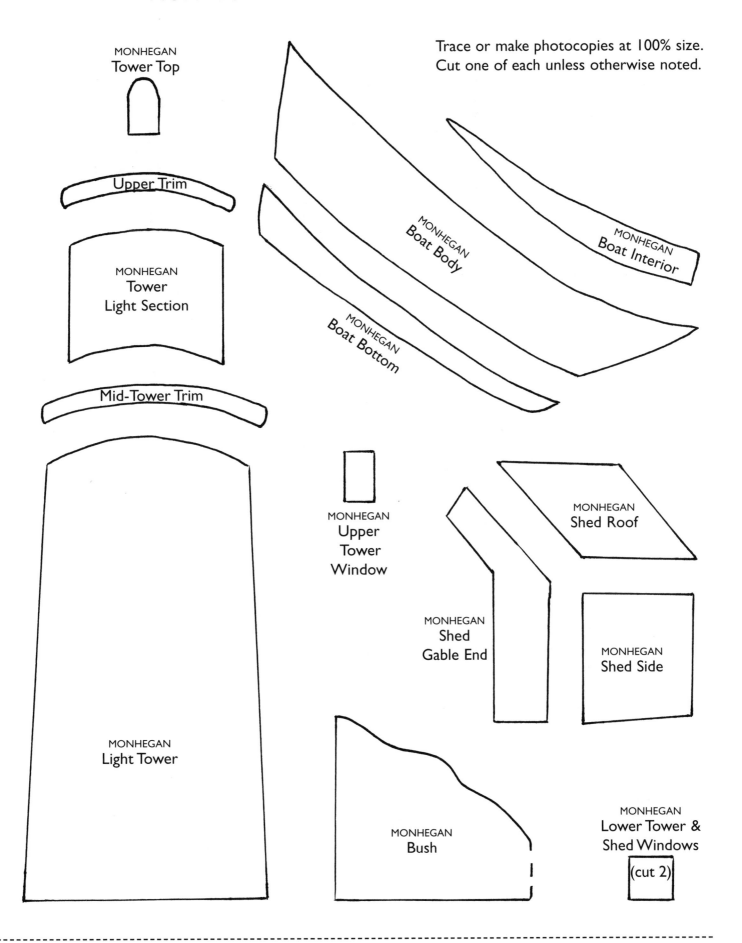

MONHEGAN
Tower Top

Trace or make photocopies at 100% size.
Cut one of each unless otherwise noted.

Upper Trim

MONHEGAN
Boat Body

MONHEGAN
Boat Interior

MONHEGAN
Tower
Light Section

MONHEGAN
Boat Bottom

Mid-Tower Trim

MONHEGAN
Upper
Tower
Window

MONHEGAN
Shed Roof

MONHEGAN
Shed
Gable End

MONHEGAN
Shed Side

MONHEGAN
Light Tower

MONHEGAN
Bush

MONHEGAN
Lower Tower &
Shed Windows

(cut 2)

Rockland Breakwater Light

*M*aine's "Lime City" was an important seaport during shipping's heyday. Limestone from area quarries and seafood from surrounding waters were shipped from Rockland to faraway places. Many famous buildings were constructed of Maine granite.

While Rockland's harbor was deep and wide, it offered little protection from the sea. In 1888, the government built a short breakwater with a trapezoid-shaped light tower at the end. Just as the term implies, such a jetty is meant to break the onslaught of waves sweeping in from the open sea.

During the ensuing years, the original barrier was periodically lengthened with additional massive blocks of cut stone. This continuing construction was dependent upon intermittant funding, and the project moved slowly. Finally, the breakwater was finished in 1902, extending a mile across the entrance to the harbor, and a significantly more durable light tower and lighthouse keeper's dwelling were built at the end.

The lighthouse is built atop a substantial granite base. This not only increased the level of safety for the keeper, back when the light station was still manned, but also prevented deterioration from the sea. During the extra high tides of spring and fall, waves continuously churn over the breakwater, swirling around the light station's sturdy foundation.

Rockland Breakwater Light's fourth-order Fresnel lens flashes its white light at five-second intervals and can be seen for twenty-four miles.

*T*his square affords a close-up view of the lighthouse and tower. The design requires patience to assemble, but its interesting perspective and bright colors make a stunning square.

Materials Needed

Fabrics:

    6½" x 12½" sky piece
    6½" x 12½" sea piece
    1½" X 12½" breakwater piece (brown)
    White for house and left end of granite base
    Reds for brick tower, ell, door, and two chimneys
    Dark gray for roofs
    Black for tower trim pieces
    Medium gray for granite base
    Green for island
    Check for light section
    Gray print for windows

Black embroidery floss for tower trim

Assembling the Square

Review the directions below before beginning this square. You will first assemble the background, then the tower from the base up, and then the ell and house.

1. Prepare pieces for appliqué (p. 7, "How to Appliqué," steps 1–4), referring to the photograph to determine which edges to leave flat because they will be overlapped by other pieces.

2. Baste island piece to sky piece, matching sides and bottoms. Slip-stitch in place.

3. Using a ¼-inch seam allowance, stitch sky piece to sea piece.

4. Draw slightly uneven lines across top and bottom of breakwater piece. Using lines as a guide, fold under and baste. Pin piece to background 1¾ inches from the bottom.

5. Stitch white granite base left end piece to gray granite base piece. Fit base behind breakwater and pin.

6. Working from bottom to top, construct the lighthouse tower. Pin pieces in place.

7. Pin brick ell and ell roof to background. The left side of roof will eventually fit over front of house section. Fit bottom of ell behind breakwater.

8. Next, build the house. Add gambrel roof—lower section, then upper—to house.

9. Pin chimneys, dormer, doors, and windows in place.

10. Adjust pieces as needed. When placement is satisfactory, baste everything.

11. Slip-stitch all pieces in place. Press.

12. Using 2 strands of floss, add the tower trim details (refer to the Burnt Island Light quilt square photo).

13. Press the finished square.

If the square is to be part of a larger project such as a bedcover or wall hanging, set it aside until you assemble the project.

For a single-square project such as a tote bag or pillow, make a sandwich of completed lighthouse square, batting, and backing. Baste together. Complete your quilt project according to the directions in the "Projects, Projects, Projects" chapter.

Quilting Suggestions

Outline quilt around all pieces. Using masking tape, quilt parallel lines for granite blocks on granite base and shingle lines on roofs. Quilt waves on sea. Quilt two clouds in left sky. (Cloud patterns can be found on page 103.)

QUILT SQUARE. FOR COLOR PHOTOGRAPH, SEE P. 70.

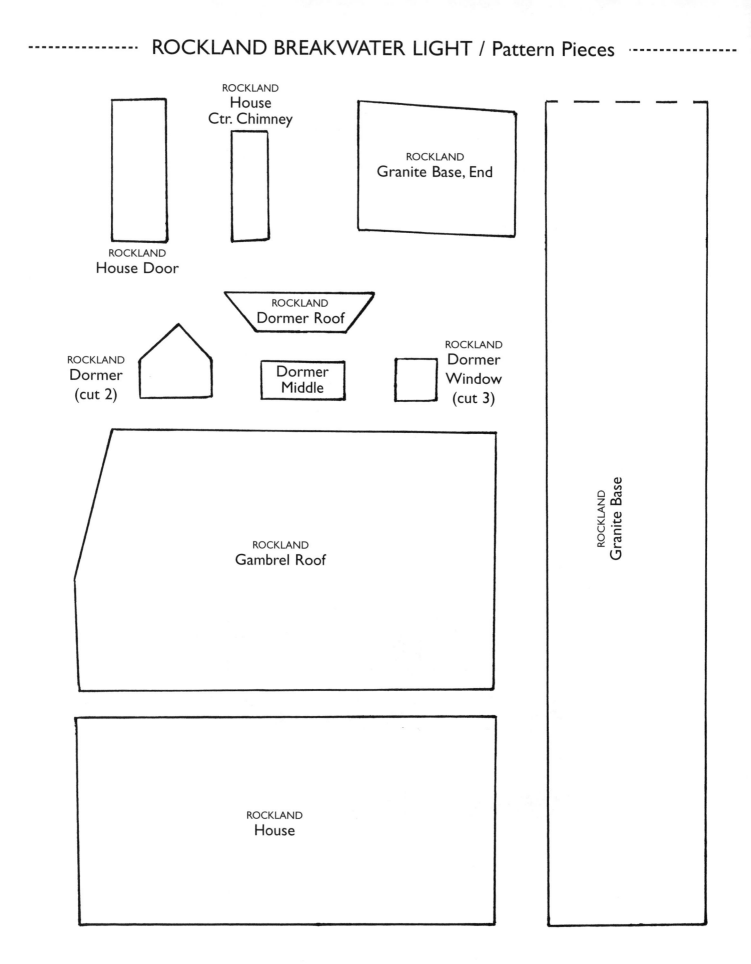

ROCKLAND
House
Ctr. Chimney

ROCKLAND
Granite Base, End

ROCKLAND
House Door

ROCKLAND
Dormer Roof

ROCKLAND
Dormer
(cut 2)

Dormer
Middle

ROCKLAND
Dormer
Window
(cut 3)

ROCKLAND
Gambrel Roof

ROCKLAND
Granite Base

ROCKLAND
House

Trace or make photocopy at 100% size. Cut one of each unless otherwise noted.

Solid lines are stitching lines. When cutting, add ⅛" to ¼" outside of lines for seam allowance. Dashed lines are cutting lines for edges that will align with edge of quilt square.

For cloud patterns see p. 103.

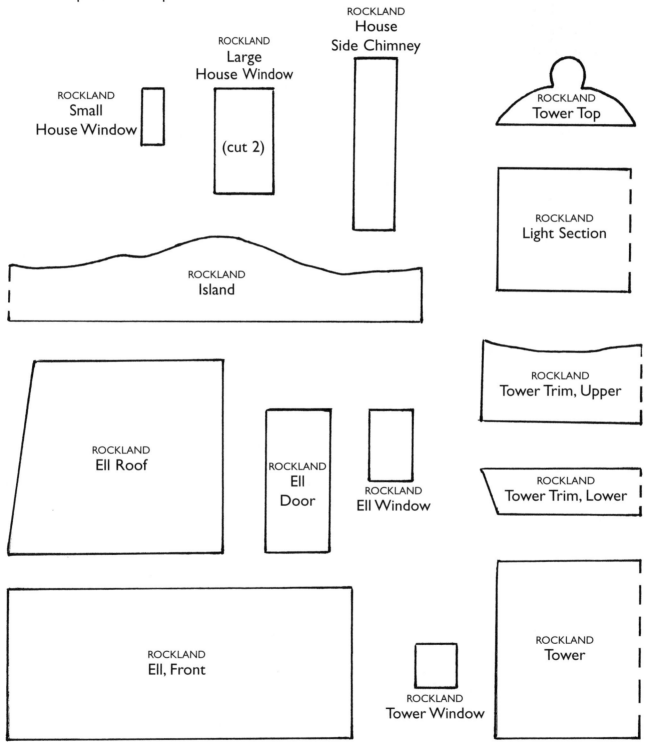

Seguin Island Light

In 1607, an approaching storm forced captains George Popham and Gilbert Raleigh to seek shelter off a small island near the mouth of a river. When the gale subsided, the crew rowed to the mainland and built dwellings. That colony, Fort St. George—later renamed Fort Popham—was the first English settlement in North America. The tiny settlement lasted but a single year.

One hundred eighty-eight years would pass before a light tower was erected on the small island, situated two miles south of the mouth of the "gallant river," now known as the Kennebec. The island was named Seguin, from the Indian word sutquin, meaning, "the place where the sea vomits"—an apt description of the sea's behavior in this spot. When the wind blows hard onshore and outgoing tides are moving swiftly in the opposite direction, fierce rip tides can result. A mariner must be vigilant in order to safely navigate here.

In the early days of the new republic, traffic was heavy on both the Kennebec and Sheepscot rivers. There was an urgent need for a beacon to guide marine traffic. In 1795, Maine's second lighthouse was built on Seguin Island. (Portland Head Light, Maine's oldest, had been completed in 1791.) Seguin's first wooden tower was replaced in 1819 with a stone structure, and rebuilt once more in 1858. This 53-foot cut-stone tower stands 186 feet above mean high water, making Seguin the most elevated light along the Maine coast.

With a fixed white beam reaching twenty miles seaward, Seguin is equipped with the only first-order Fresnel lens in Maine, and one of only two first-order lenses in all of New England. Reflectors are positioned to send all the light seaward. The land side of the light remains in darkness. After the light was automated, the Coast Guard twice made plans to remove the giant lens but was prevented by a groundswell of public opposition. Following many protests, requests, and petitions, the lens—worth more than eight million dollars—was allowed to remain in place.

Seguin holds the record for being the foggiest light station in the country. In 1907, the haunting sound of its fog signal was heard for nearly one third of the year. It was not the first U.S. light station to receive a fog bell; that honor went to West Quoddy Head (p. 78). Seguin's first fog bell was barely audible and was replaced by another in 1853. Later, there was a stream-driven whistle, followed by a diaphone horn. Many stories attest to the intensity of that horn. There are those who claim to have heard it in Bath, some fourteen miles upriver. One light keeper said that vibrations from the signal would knock sea gulls from mid-air.

When Seguin Island Light was built, the 22-acre island was heavily wooded. This wood supplied heat for the keeper's dwelling for many years. Today, the island is nearly barren.

There are those who believe that ghosts roam the island, and several light keepers have experienced strange happenings there. Some have reported hearing a young girl laughing as she frolics about the premises. One ghost who seems to wander freely in his oilskins and sou'wester is called Old Captain.

A legend concerning buried treasure persisted for years. To put an end to them, the government hired a man to search the entire island for the mythical hoard. After nine fruitless months, the treasure hunter proclaimed the rumor to be false.

Seguin Island Light was fully automated in 1985, and it looked as if the keeper's house and outbuildings were doomed to suffer the usual fate of unoccupied buildings: slowly rotting away once there was nobody there to care for them. Fortunately, however, the Friends of Seguin organization was established in 1986 to restore and maintain this historic site.

The Seguin Island Light Station has several outbuildings, which could conceivably become a quilter's nightmare. Therefore, this square is designed according to the concept of "less is more," and features only the tower top, with its massive Fresnel lens, standing tall against the heavens.

Materials Needed

Fabrics:

12½" x 12½" sky piece
White for tower and tower trim
Black for trim around glass section
Gray check for tower window
Yellow for Fresnel lens

Black embroidery floss for trim around tower and light

Assembling the Square

You will assemble the tower from the bottom up, then apply the trim pieces.

1. Prepare pieces for appliqué (p.7, "How to Appliqué," steps 1–4). Fold and baste only the sides of the lower tower. Fold and baste sides and top of mid-tower. Fold and baste sides of Fresnel lens piece.

2. Find centers of background square and lower tower piece. Center the tower.

3. Working from bottom to top, pin and baste each tower piece to background, fitting bottom of mid-tower behind lower tower, etc.

4. Using tower glass section guide as a marker, fit Fresnel lens piece in place behind mid-tower piece. Pin and baste.

5. Pin and baste tower top in place; slip-stitch.

6. Now, pin and baste tower bottom trim and tower glass section trim in the proper places. Baste window on lower tower; slip-stitch.

7. Press.

8. Using 2 strands of floss, add the trim details on

QUILT SQUARE. FOR COLOR PHOTOGRAPH, SEE P. 24.

tower trim and around the light section (refer to the Seguin Island Light quilt square photograph).

9. Press the finished square.

If the square is to be part of a larger project such as a bedcover or wall hanging, set it aside until you assemble the project. For a single-square project such as a tote bag or pillow, make a sandwich of completed lighthouse square, batting, and backing. Baste.

Complete project according to the directions in the "Projects, Projects, Projects" chapter.

Quilting Suggestions

Using ¾-inch masking tape, quilt tower blocks on lower tower section. Stagger the blocks on alternating rows. Quilt panes on window. Outline quilt around tower and tower pieces.

Trace or make photocopy at 100% size.

Solid lines are stitching lines. When cutting, add ⅛" to ¼" outside of lines for seam allowance. Dashed lines are cutting lines for edges that will align with edge of quilt square.

Cut one of each.

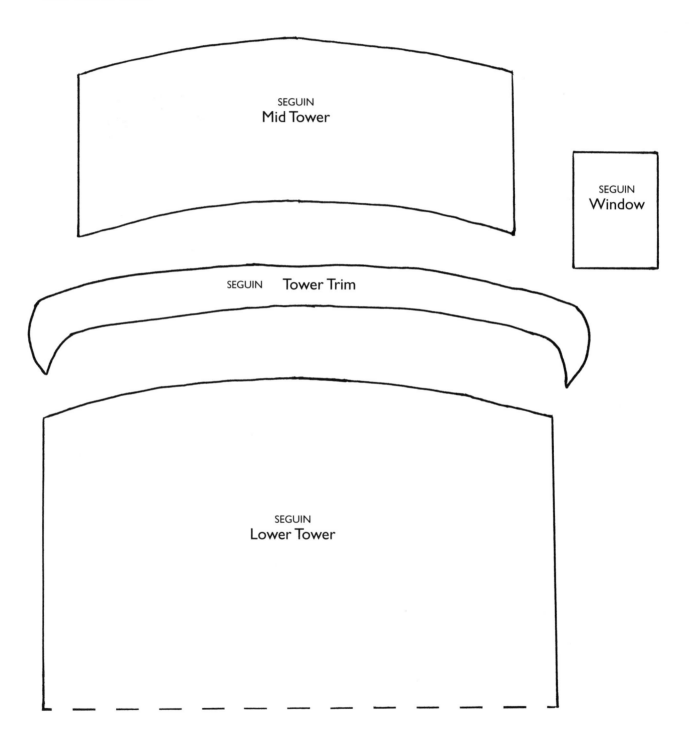

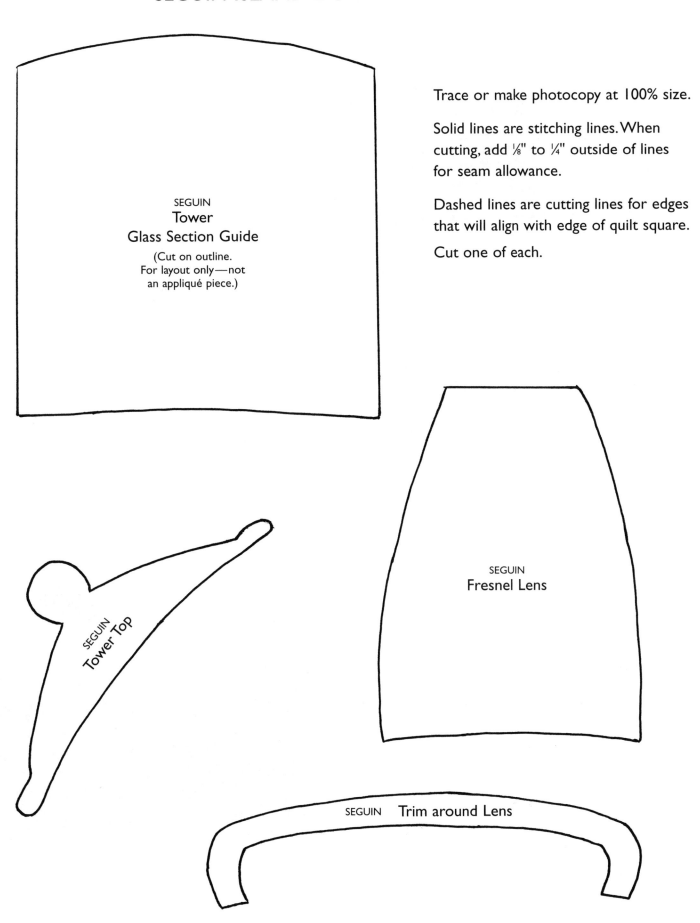

SEGUIN
Tower
Glass Section Guide
(Cut on outline.
For layout only—not
an appliqué piece.)

Trace or make photocopy at 100% size.

Solid lines are stitching lines. When cutting, add ⅛" to ¼" outside of lines for seam allowance.

Dashed lines are cutting lines for edges that will align with edge of quilt square.

Cut one of each.

SEGUIN
Tower Top

SEGUIN
Fresnel Lens

SEGUIN   **Trim around Lens**

West Quoddy Head Light

*I*n Lubec, Maine, West Quoddy Head Light sits on the east-ernmost point of land in the continental United States. That's about as far down east as one can get.

New Englanders used to speak of going "down to Maine" and "up to Boston." (In fact, many people still use those ex-pressions.) At first, these phrases make no sense, but if one considers that folks once traveled between Boston and Maine via water, the meaning becomes clear. Since the prevailing fair-weather winds come from the southwest, one traveled downwind to Maine and upwind to Boston. Today, when Maine people speak of "down east," they are referring to the coastal region beginning roughly at Ellsworth, Maine, and extending into New Brunswick, Canada.

Standing eighty-three feet above mean high water, West Quoddy Head Light looks out over the Bay of Fundy. Its welcoming white beacon flashes twice every fifteen seconds, sending a beam eighteen miles seaward. Its signature red and white stripes are famous, although we do not know when they were first painted on the tower. The original rubblestone tower was built in 1807, and replaced in 1858 with the pres-ent forty-nine-foot brick tower.

In 1820, the first fog bell in the nation was installed here, although other light stations were plagued by more fog. The West Quoddy Head lightkeeper struck the bell by hand, a tedious job during extended periods of fog. Not surprisingly, he complained persistently about this, and in 1827 the govern-ment allotted him an additional seventy dollars a year for his efforts. Added to his $300.00 annual salary, this meant the

light keeper earned about $7.11 per week (plus his housing and uniforms, of course).

Despite the keepers' valiant efforts, that original bell and the three that later replaced it were not very effective. The sig-nal still could not be heard. The bells were eventually replaced by a powerful diaphone horn.

West Quoddy's third-order Fresnel lens still guides fishing vessels and pleasure boats into Lubec Channel. The light was automated in 1988.

QUILT SQUARE. FOR COLOR PHOTOGRAPH, SEE P. 24.

Although this square does not represent the most typical view of West Quoddy Head Light, and some artistic license has been taken with tree placement, the scale of the tower and the small building are proportionately correct.

Materials Needed

Fabrics:

6" x 12½" sky piece
4½" x 12½" sea piece
3" x 12½" medium green for mid-ground piece
Tower stripes: 5" x 6" red piece and 4⅜" x 6"
   white piece
Red for tower top and shed roof
White for shed
Black for mid-tower
Yellow for light
Dark color for shed window
Brown for tree trunks
2 shades of green for trees
Pale green for distant land
Gray for foreground ledge

Black embroidery floss for trim on tower and light

Assembling the Square

You will first build the striped lighthouse tower, then assemble the background square and appliqué the lighthouse, trees, and foreground ledge onto the background.

1. To assemble tower stripes, cut 8 red strips and 7 white strips, each measuring 6 inches long by ⅝ inch wide. With right sides together and alternating colors, stitch along the long edges. Start and end with a red stripe. Press.

2. Place tower pattern on the right side of this striped cloth and trace around it. Cut outside the traced line to give a ¼-inch seam allowance all around.

3. Prepare pieces for appliqué (p. 7, "How to Appliqué," steps 1–4), referring to the photograph to determine which

edges to leave flat because they will be overlapped by other pieces.

4. Assemble the sky section: Place the wrong side of the distant land pieces onto the right side of the sky piece, matching and basting along bottoms. Slip-stitch the top.

5. Next, assemble the sea section: Stitch mid-ground piece to water piece using a ¼-inch seam. Stitch this to the sky section, forming the background square.

6. On the bottom left of the square, appliqué the foreground ledge piece onto the mid-ground piece.

7. Position remaining pieces on the background. To assemble trees, start with the trunk and work up to the top, arranging each section to fit over the top of the previous piece. Place the smaller tree slightly behind the larger one.

8. Pin, baste, and slip-stitch in place.

9. Press.

10. Using 2 strands of floss, add the trim details on tower and light (refer to the West Quoddy Head Light quilt square photograph).

11. Press the finished square.

If the square is to be part of a larger project such as a bedcover or wall hanging, set it aside until you assemble the project.

For a single-square project such as a tote bag or pillow, make a sandwich of completed lighthouse square, batting, and backing. Baste together. Complete your quilt project according to the directions in the "Projects, Projects, Projects" chapter.

Quilting Suggestions

Outline-stitch around tower, shed, window, trees, ledge, and distant land. Quilt two clouds in sky. Quilt four wave lines on sea. (Cloud and wave patterns can be found on pages 103 and 102.) This appealing square is now ready to use in a finished project.

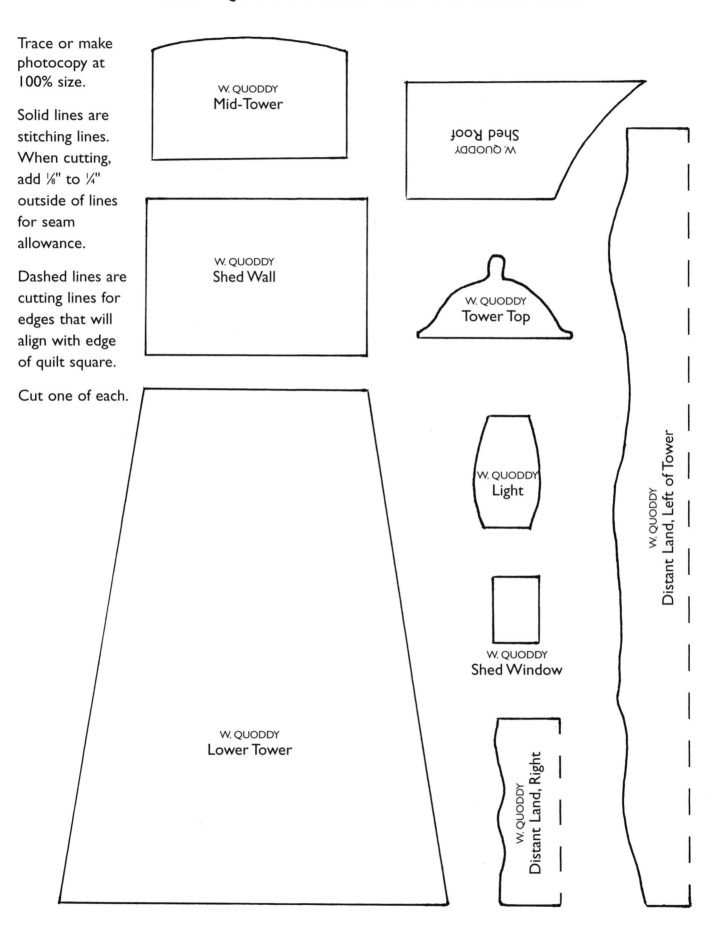

Trace or make photocopy at 100% size.

Solid lines are stitching lines. When cutting, add ⅛" to ¼" outside of lines for seam allowance.

Dashed lines are cutting lines for edges that will align with edge of quilt square.

Cut one of each.

W. QUODDY
Mid-Tower

W. QUODDY
Shed Roof

W. QUODDY
Shed Wall

W. QUODDY
Tower Top

W. QUODDY
Light

W. QUODDY
Shed Window

W. QUODDY
Lower Tower

W. QUODDY
Distant Land, Right

W. QUODDY
Distant Land, Left of Tower

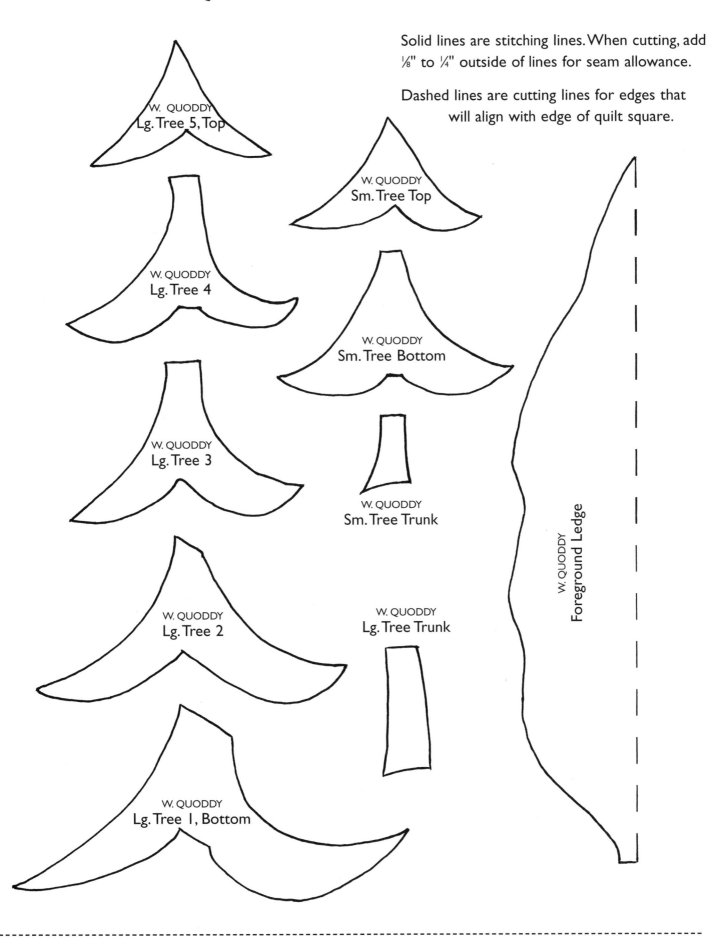

Solid lines are stitching lines. When cutting, add ⅛" to ¼" outside of lines for seam allowance.

Dashed lines are cutting lines for edges that will align with edge of quilt square.

W. QUODDY
Lg. Tree 5, Top

W. QUODDY
Sm. Tree Top

W. QUODDY
Lg. Tree 4

W. QUODDY
Sm. Tree Bottom

W. QUODDY
Lg. Tree 3

W. QUODDY
Sm. Tree Trunk

W. QUODDY
Lg. Tree 2

W. QUODDY
Lg. Tree Trunk

W. QUODDY
Foreground Ledge

W. QUODDY
Lg. Tree 1, Bottom

Stars to Steer By

In the early days, stars were the sailor's friends. They not only helped navigators determine a ship's position but also symbolized clear skies and thus fair weather.

This versatile star pattern can be used singly or in multiples, as on this pillow example. The appliquéd stars may be invisibly slip-stitched in place or attached with fusible webbing and edged with decorative blanket stitch. Both of these techniques are explained in the "Achievable Appliqué" chapter, beginning on page 7.

The star pattern also works well for "just plain quilting," as noted on the next page.

Materials Needed

For the basic square:
  12½" x 12½" background color square
  Various small prints for appliqué stars
  12½" x 12½" backing material square

For optional fusible appliqué technique:
  Fusible webbing
  Black embroidery floss for blanket stitching
  Decorative button for each star (optional)

If square is for a pillow:
  ½ yard additional fabric for pillow ruffle or cording

Assembling the Square

For the slip-stitched appliqué technique, follow the directions given on page 7. For appliqué using fusible webbing and decorative blanket stitching, follow the directions on page 8.

If the square is to be part of a larger project such as a bedcover or wall hanging, set the finished square aside until you assemble the project.

For a single-square project such as a tote bag or pillow, make a sandwich of completed Star square, batting, and backing. Baste, then quilt.

Complete your project according to the directions in the "Projects, Projects, Projects" chapter. (To make a ruffled pillow like the one shown here, follow the directions for "Picture Perfect Pillows" on p. 13.)

Quilting Suggestions

If you attached your stars using fusible webbing, there is no need to do quilting. Simply attach the decorative buttons by going through all three layers, and this will hold the batting in place.

If you used the slip-stitch appliqué technique, quilt one or several rows around each star. The first row should be close to the star. All other rows should be ¼ inch apart. (You could also add buttons to the center of these stars, as described in the paragraph above, and eliminate the need for quilting.)

"Just Plain Quilting" Version

Use the star pattern template as a stitching guide. Quilt around each star using two strands of embroidery floss or one strand of quilting thread.

Basic Star Pattern

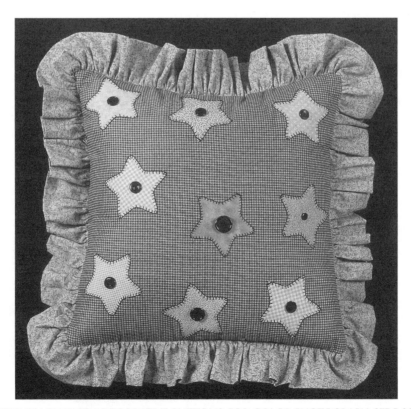

STAR PILLOW WITH DECORATIVE BUTTONS. FOR COLOR PHOTOGRAPH, SEE P. 28.

Those Pesky Crows

I learned many interesting facts while researching this book, but the one that truly tickled my Yankee funny bone had to do with "ridding the island of a pest of crows." When Islesboro became an incorporated town, the citizens decided to eliminate the island's overwhelming crow population by offering a bounty of twelve cents per dead crow plus a two-dollar bonus at year's end for the person who had eliminated the largest number of the raucous black creatures. Since I have a love/hate relationship with these tantalizing, shiny birds, and since they are part of the coastal landscape, a design with a crow and a lighthouse seemed appropriate for this book.

This pattern can be either slip-stitch appliquéd or made using fusible webbing (with or without the decorative blanket stitching). It works perfectly for a large pillow or small wall hanging. ***For a color photo, see page 25.***

Materials for a 17" x 20" Finished Patch

Fabrics needed:

6½" x 20½" sky piece
9½" x 20½" sea piece
2½" x 20½" beach piece
Black for crow
White for lighthouse
Red for door, windows, and tower
Small check for tower light section
4 shades of green for trees
Another green for grassy land
2 shades of gray for fence posts and lighthouse ledge

For fusible appliqué technique:

Fusible webbing
Black embroidery floss for blanket stitching (optional)
Yellow star-shaped button for light (optional)

Assembling the Patch

1. Cut out pieces: Cut **on** the outlines for fusible appliqué; cut ⅛" to ¼" **outside** lines for traditional applique.

2. If using traditional appliqué, prepare pieces as described on page 7, steps 1–4.

3. Construct the background by stitching sky, sea, and beach pieces together using a ¼-inch seam allowance. Press.

4. Using the picture as a guide, arrange the pieces on background. To secure them, follow directions on page 7 for slip-stitch appliqué, or page 8 if using fusible webbing and blanket stitching.

5. Finish the project you have chosen for this patch by referring to the "Projects, Projects, Projects" chapter.

Quilting for Traditional Appliqué Version

Outline quilt (one row) or shadow quilt (several rows) around each piece. Stitch branch patterns on trees. Quilt wave patterns on sea and a cloud outline in sky.

EXAMPLE WITH DECORATIVE BLANKET STITCHING

Trace or make photocopy at 100% size.

For traditional slip-stitch appliqué, add ⅛" to ¼" outside of lines (for seam allowance) when cutting.

For fusible appliqué technique, cut on outlines, with no added seam allowance.

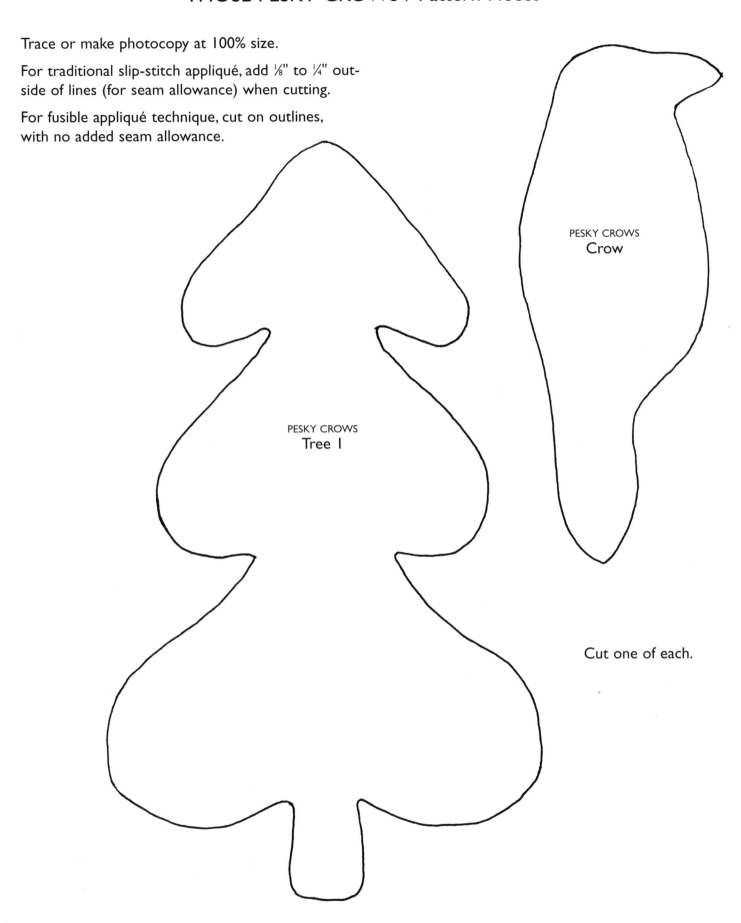

PESKY CROWS
Crow

PESKY CROWS
Tree 1

Cut one of each.

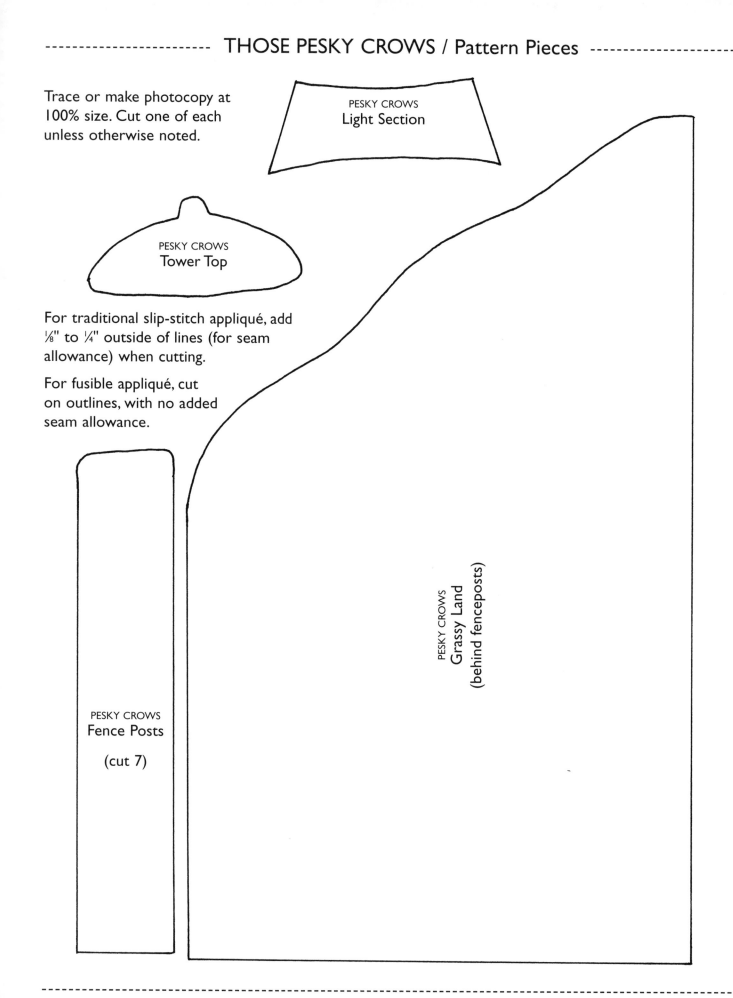

Trace or make photocopy at
100% size. Cut one of each
unless otherwise noted.

PESKY CROWS
Light Section

PESKY CROWS
Tower Top

For traditional slip-stitch appliqué, add
⅛" to ¼" outside of lines (for seam
allowance) when cutting.

For fusible appliqué, cut
on outlines, with no added
seam allowance.

PESKY CROWS
Fence Posts

(cut 7)

PESKY CROWS
Grassy Land
(behind fenceposts)

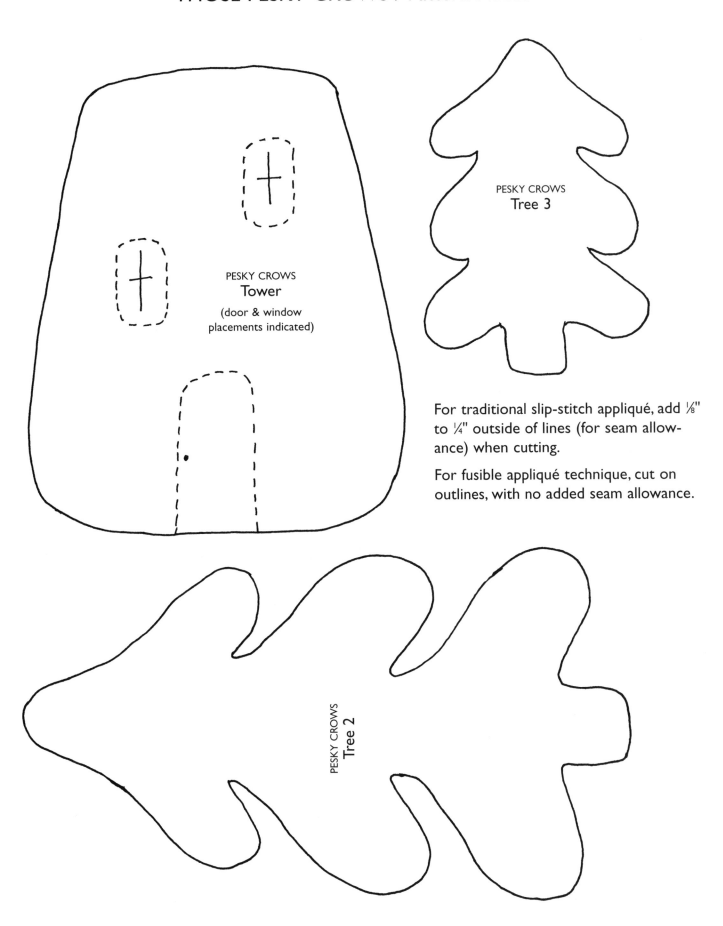

PESKY CROWS
Tree 3

PESKY CROWS
Tower
(door & window
placements indicated)

For traditional slip-stitch appliqué, add ⅛"
to ¼" outside of lines (for seam allowance) when cutting.

For fusible appliqué technique, cut on
outlines, with no added seam allowance.

PESKY CROWS
Tree 2

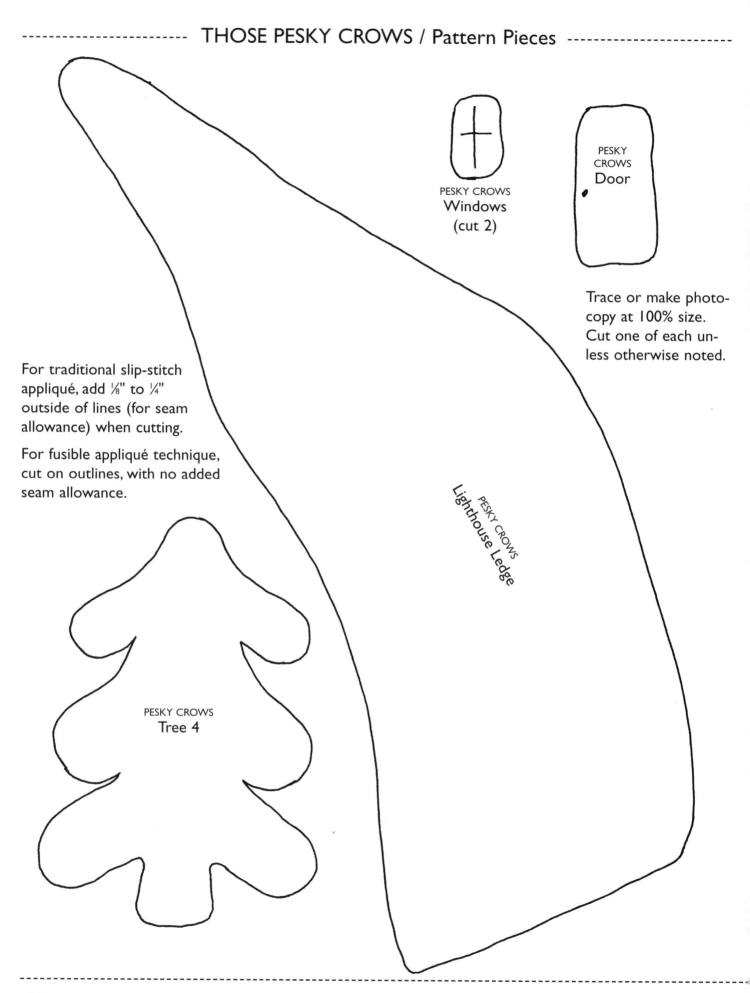

PESKY CROWS
Windows
(cut 2)

PESKY
CROWS
Door

Trace or make photo-
copy at 100% size.
Cut one of each un-
less otherwise noted.

For traditional slip-stitch
appliqué, add ⅛" to ¼"
outside of lines (for seam
allowance) when cutting.

For fusible appliqué technique,
cut on outlines, with no added
seam allowance.

PESKY CROWS
Lighthouse Ledge

PESKY CROWS
Tree 4

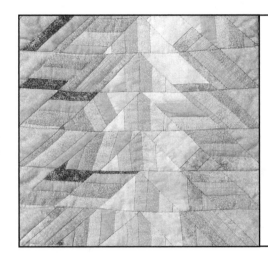

Kaleidoscopic Fresnel

*E*arly lighthouse lamps were fueled by whale oil until the decline of the whaling industry. Lard oil was also popular. After the mid-nineteenth century, burners were designed to use vaporized mineral oil. Kerosene was the final fuel choice.

In 1822, French physicist Augustin Fresnel invented a lens consisting of hundreds of prisms fitted together in a metal frame. These prismatic lenses—which resemble giant glass beehives—were designed to pick up every bit of light from the lamp inside, concentrating each small beam into one powerful beacon visible from miles away. Its expert design makes the Fresnel lens as effective today as it was nearly two hundred years ago.

Early Fresnel lenses were hand ground and polished by workmen for pennies a day. Today, if a Fresnel becomes damaged, another optic is used, since replacing the original would cost millions.

Fresnel lenses come in six sizes, ranging from first to sixth order. The giant first-order lenses are six or more feet in diameter and may be as tall as twelve feet. A sixth-order lens is about one foot in diameter. First-, second-, and third-order lenses were used mainly in coastal lighthouses. Fourth-, fifth-, and sixth-order lenses were more efficient for harbor and river lights.

*F*resnel lenses are designed to best radiate tower lights after dark. During daylight hours, the prisms of the lens mirror the sun's rays, forming beautiful rainbow reflections. This design represents those prismatic colors.

There is no right or wrong method of piecing placement in this design. Just as prisms do not repeat reflections, each quilter's square will take on a different perspective. It is fun to see different designs emerge.

I used this square as the pocket for a tote bag, but it would also make a delightful baby quilt, especially if bright colors were used for the rainbow strips.

Although the design looks complicated and the directions appear lengthy, it actually is a very easy square to make. ***For a color photograph, see p. 31.***

Materials Needed for 12½" x 12½" Square

⅛ yard each of three different shades of yellow

⅛ yard each of six rainbow colors (may be either bold or subtle shades)

½ yard light blue sky material (this is enough for the backing piece as well)

Assembling the Square

1. Cut two 1¼-inch strips from each of the three yellows. Sew each pair of strips together to create one long strip for each shade of yellow. Cut the long strips so they measure 55 inches long.

2. Follow the same process with each of your 6 rainbow colors. Repeat the steps with one of the colors. You will end up with a total of 7 rainbow-color strips.

3. From the light blue material, cut two strips each measuring 2½ inches x 55 inches (as you did with the yellow and rainbow strips above, you will have to sew strips together in order to get the 55-inch length). Also cut one 12½" x 12½" backing square and (using pattern pieces) 12 **small triangles**.

4. Arrange 3 rainbow colors in one group and stitch together along the long sides, using a ¼-inch seam allowance. Arrange 4 rainbow colors in a second group (repeating one color from group 1) and stitch together (sketch 1). Press.

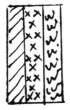

SKETCH 1

5. Stitch the 3 yellow strips together (sketch 2). Press.

6. Stitch the 3-strip rainbow group to one of the sky strips (sketch 3).

SKETCH 2

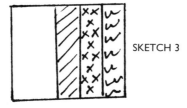

SKETCH 3

7. Now, stitch the yellow group to the rainbow end of the strip just completed in step 6.

8. Stitch the remaining sky strip to the right side of the yellow end of the strip just completed in step 7. Finish by stitching the 4-color rainbow strip to that second sky strip (sketch 4). Press.

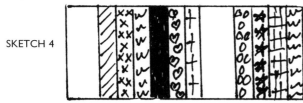

SKETCH 4

9. Using the pattern templates on p. 91, randomly cut 12 **left diagonal** and 12 **right diagonal** pieces from the rainbow-colors portion of the large strip. Each diagonal piece is supposed to be unique and not match any other. Cut some of them vertically and some horizontally. It is all right to have a bit of sky material in the diagonals. Just remember, there are definite left and right patterns, and you will need 12 of each.

10. Cut 6 **large triangles** from the center yellow/sky section of the assembled strip. Don't cut them all the same; instead, stagger the placement of the pattern piece so that the yellows will fall at a slightly different place within each triangle. (Sketch 5 shows one triangle).

SKETCH 5

11. Lay out the Fresnel square, moving pieces around until the overall design pleases you. The Fresnel square consists of 6 horizontal bands. Each band has a large triangle in the center, flanked by 2 left diagonals and 2 right diagonals. A small sky triangle on each end completes the band (sketch 6).

SKETCH 6

12. Stitch the pieces in the first band together. Set that band back in place. Repeat with the other 5 bands.

13. Once all 6 bands have been stitched, trim each one. Stitch the bands together to form the square. Press.

If the square is to be part of a larger project such as a bedcover or wall hanging, set it aside until you assemble the project. For a single-square project such as a tote bag or pillow, make a sandwich of the completed Fresnel square, batting, and backing. Baste together.

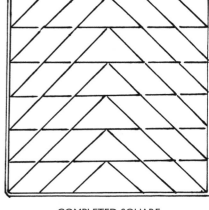

COMPLETED SQUARE

Complete your project according to the directions in the "Projects, Projects, Projects" chapter. To make a tote bag, follow directions on page 14.

Quilting Suggestion

You can either work the quilting stitches in the ditch between the separate colors or quilt an overall swirl-type design.

Trace or make photocopy at 100% size.

Outer line is <u>cutting</u> line.
Inner line is <u>seam</u> line (with ¼" seam allowance).

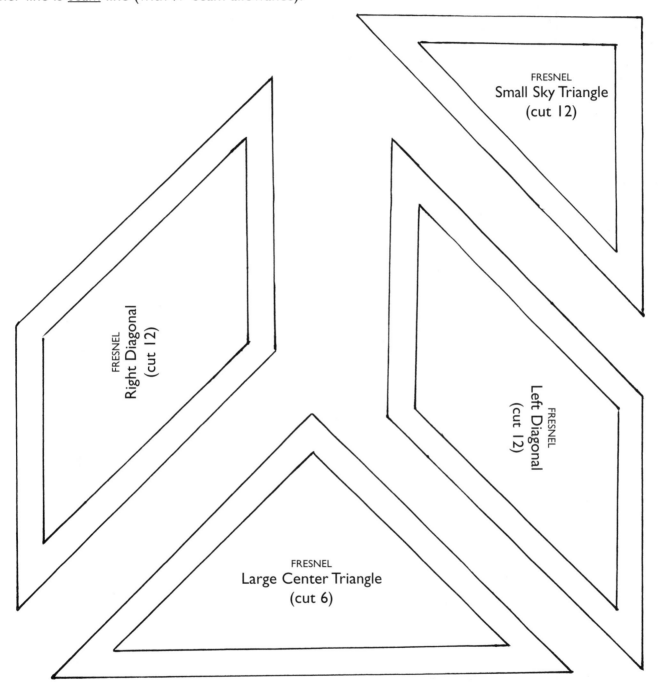

FRESNEL
Small Sky Triangle
(cut 12)

FRESNEL
Right Diagonal
(cut 12)

FRESNEL
Left Diagonal
(cut 12)

FRESNEL
Large Center Triangle
(cut 6)

A Patchwork Schooner

*L*ighthouses were important to the schooners of yesteryear, which hauled cargo all along the Atlantic seaboard. Many schooners had two or three masts, but the largest ones had five or six masts, and one behemoth built in Waldoboro, Maine, had seven!

This design is a variation of an old pattern. For realism, you might choose green for the ship's hull, white for the sails, and blues for water and sky, but this design works well in fanciful colors, too. *(See p. 27 for photo of one color combination.)* If you plan to combine Patchwork Schooner squares with lighthouse squares in a large project, use some of the same prints in both.

Fabrics Needed (for 4 quilt squares)

¼ yard each of 4 different prints—for sky, sails, ship's hull, and sea

Cut (for 1 quilt square)

6 sky triangles
6 sail triangles
2 sea triangles
2 ship triangles
1 ship square

Assembling the Square

1. Stitch one sky triangle to one sail, forming a 4-inch square. Repeat 5 more times.

2. Stitch one sea triangle to one ship triangle. Repeat one more time.

3. Form the top row of the square by stitching 3 sail/sky triangles together (sketch 1). Repeat once for the second row of sails.

4. Stitch one ship/sea square to each side of the ship square (sketch 2) to make the bottom row of the square.

5. Stitch these 3 rows together to complete the square (sketch 3). Press.

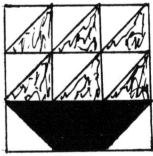

SKETCH I

SKETCH 2

SKETCH 3

If the square is to be part of a larger project such as a bedcover or wall hanging, set it aside until you assemble the project. For a single-square project such as a tote bag or pillow, make a sandwich of the completed Schooner square, batting, and backing layer. Baste together.

Complete your project according to the directions in the "Projects, Projects, Projects" chapter.

Quilting Suggestion

Place ¼-inch masking tape along the inside seam lines of a sail segment. Using the tape as a guide, quilt along the three sides of that sail piece. Repeat this with each sail piece. Then quilt around the ship's hull.

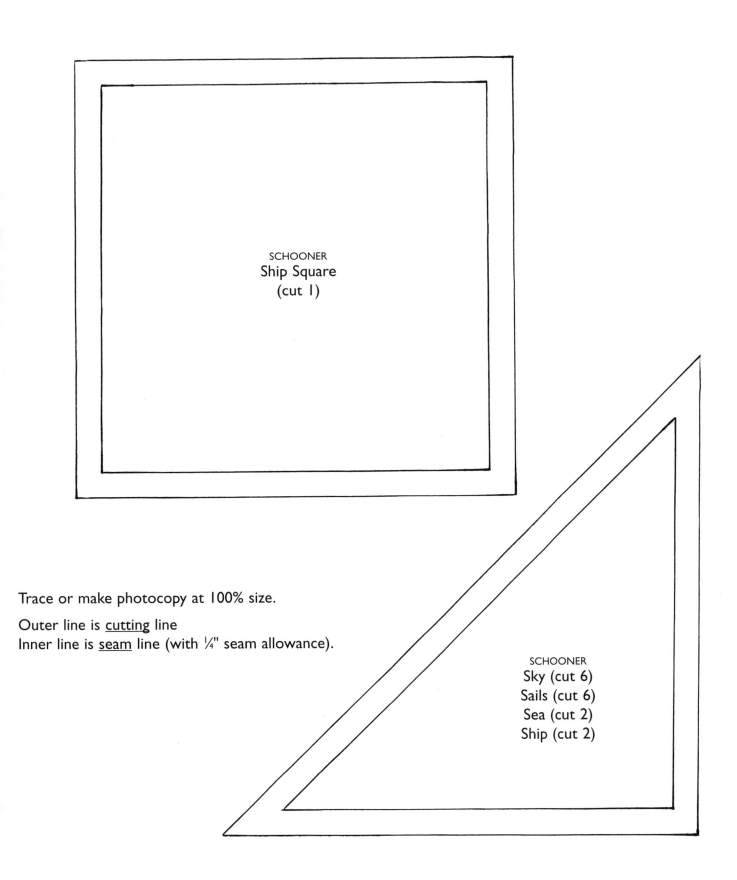

SCHOONER
Ship Square
(cut 1)

Trace or make photocopy at 100% size.

Outer line is <u>cutting</u> line
Inner line is <u>seam</u> line (with ¼" seam allowance).

SCHOONER
Sky (cut 6)
Sails (cut 6)
Sea (cut 2)
Ship (cut 2)

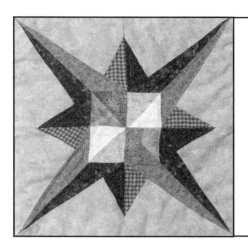

Mariner's Compass

*I*n the days of the great windjammers, mariners relied on a few instruments and their own gut feelings to get them from one point to another. One instrument of major importance was the mariner's compass.

A compass is used to determine direction. When there is nothing but sea swell and sky on the horizon, there are no landmarks to help reckon a ship's course. This is where the need for a direction finder becomes imperative. A compass contains a freely pivoting magnetic needle that always points to magnetic north.

Another aid to early navigation was the sextant. Sextants measured the angular distance needed to ascertain longitude and latitude at sea. Angles were measured using the horizon and various heavenly bodies. Using these two instruments, navigators were reasonably able to determine their position.

Area charts showing water depths and the positions of lighthouses and shoals were a necessity. Parallel rulers, rolling rulers, and protractors were used to read charts as early as the eighteenth century, and are still used today.

This patchwork mariner's compass will remind the quilter of the relationship between a mariner and his instruments. These tools—along with lighthouses, fog bells, and sheer willpower—have kept mariners on course through the centuries. Angles, measurements, instruments, and sheer will are also very much a part of the quilter's world.

*T*his square is a bit more difficult than some, but the result is worth the effort. Combine it with other squares, or allow it to stand alone in a project. *(For color photograph, see p. 26.)*

Fabrics Needed

Even though this is a geometric design, I think of the colors as representing the natural world: blues for sky and sea, gray for rocky shore, tan/brown for earth, white for clouds, etc. This color list is only a suggestion, since the compass design works well with many different combinations.

¼ yard each of the following colors:

light blue	light green	light red
dark blue	dark green	dark red
gray	tan	white

If you plan to use one of these same colors for the backing layer too, you will need an additional ½ yard of that one.

Cut

eight #1 center triangles (2 gray, 2 dark blue, 2 tan, 2 white)

four #2 major compass points (light green)

four #3 major compass points (dark green)

four #4 minor compass points (light red)

four #5 minor compass points (dark red)

four #6 background pieces (light blue)

four #7 background pieces (light blue)

Assembling the Square

Before assembling any pieces, lay out the whole quilt patch. As you work, pick up only the pieces you will be stitching and replace them in the layout as soon as you have finished with that step. By doing this, you are less apt to become confused with placements of pattern pieces and colors.

1. Stitch a dark blue #1 center triangle to a #2 major compass point, making a long, very thin triangle. Make 2 of these. Then stitch a white #1 center triangle to a light green #2 major compass point. Make 2 of these. You now have 4 **segment A triangles**.

2. Stitch a light red #4 minor compass point to a #7 background piece. Make 3 more the same way. You now have 4 **segment B triangles**.

3. Stitch one segment A to one segment B, making a large triangle (sketch 1). Repeat this step 3 more times. These are your 4 **left-side triangles**. They will form the left half of each quarter of the finished quilt patch.

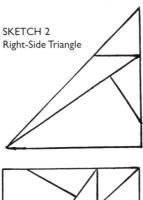

SKETCH I
Left-Side Triangle

4. Stitch a gray #1 center triangle to a dark green #3 major compass point, making another long, thin triangle. Make 2 of these. then stitch a tan #1 center triangle to a dark green #3 major compass point. Make 2 of these. You now have 4 **segment C triangles**.

5. Stitch a dark red #5 minor compass point to a #6 background piece. Make 3 more of these the same way. You now have 4 **segment D triangles.**

6. Stitch one segment C to one segment D to make a large triangle (sketch 2). Repeat this 3 more times to make 4 **right-side triangles**.

SKETCH 2
Right-Side Triangle

7. Stitch together one left-side triangle to one right-side triangle, making a square (sketch 3). Repeat this step 3 more times. You now have 4 squares, 2 with tan/white #1 center triangles, and 2 with gray/dark blue #1 center triangles

8. Stitch two squares together, matching a gray center triangle with a white center

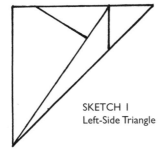

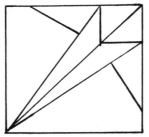

SKETCH 3

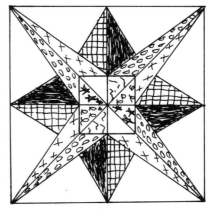

SKETCH 4

triangle (sketch 4). Repeat this step once more. You now have the two halves of the Compass.

9. Stitch the two halves together to complete the Mariner's Compass quilt square.

10. Press

If the square is to be part of a larger project such as a bedcover or wall hanging, set it aside until you assemble the project. For a single-square project such as a tote bag or pillow, make a sandwich of completed Compass square, batting, and backing. Baste.

Complete your project according to the directions in the "Projects, Projects, Projects" chapter.

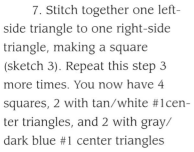

FINISHED QUILT SQUARE

Quilting Suggestion

A lot of complicated quilting would detract from this design. I recommend stitching inside each compass piece using ¼-inch masking tape as a guide. Or you may wish to simply stitch in the ditch to bring out the design.

Trace or make photocopy at 100% size.

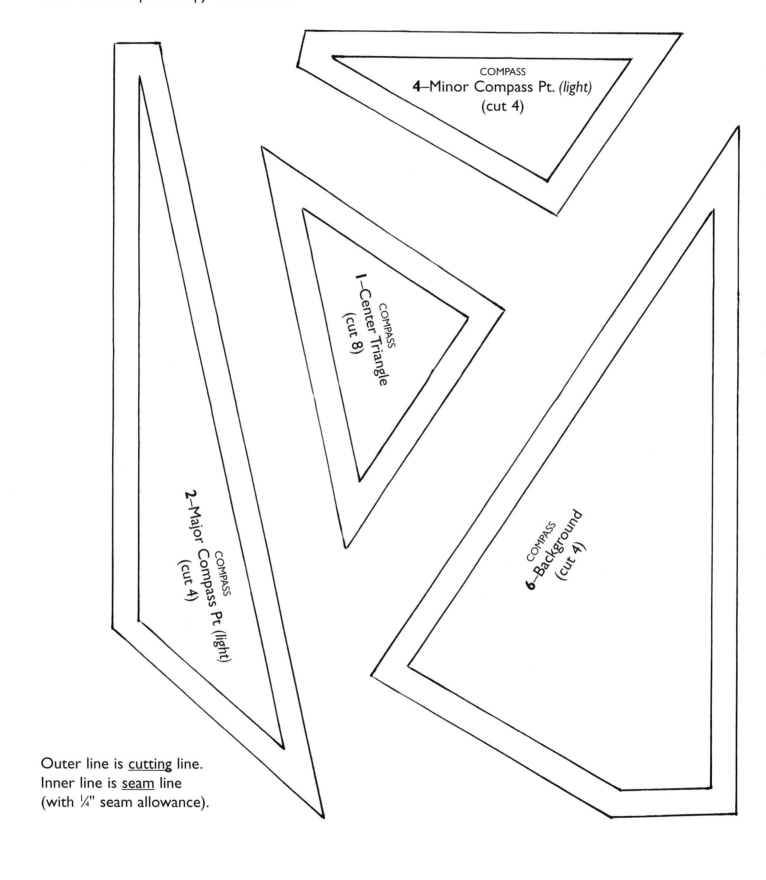

**COMPASS
4–Minor Compass Pt. *(light)*
(cut 4)**

COMPASS
**1–Center Triangle
(cut 8)**

COMPASS
**2–Major Compass Pt (light)
(cut 4)**

COMPASS
**6–Background
(cut 4)**

Outer line is <u>cutting</u> line.
Inner line is <u>seam</u> line
(with ¼" seam allowance).

Trace or make photocopy at 100% size.

Outer line is <u>cutting</u> line.
Inner line is <u>seam</u> line (with ¼" seam allowance).

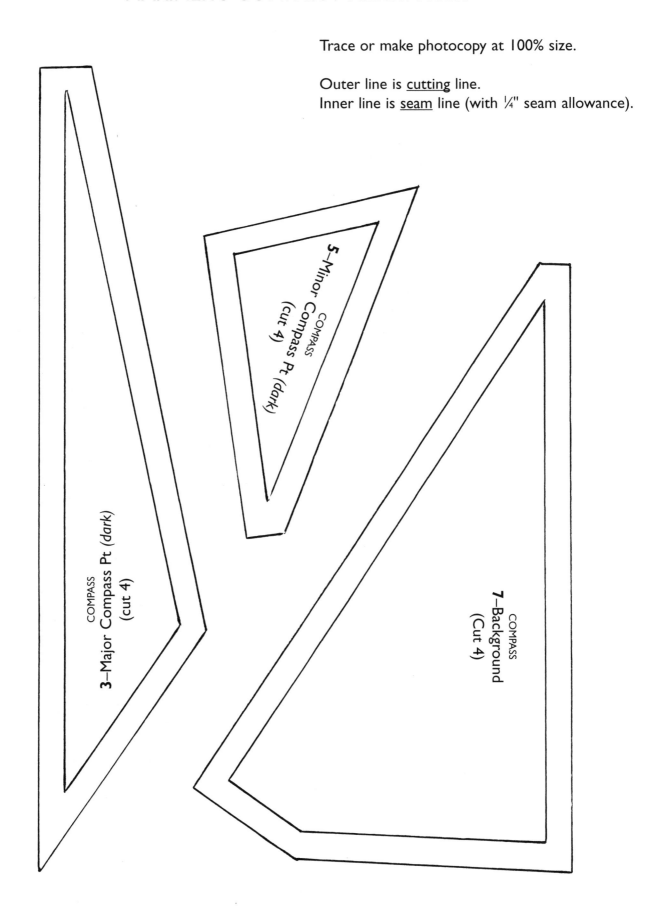

COMPASS
5–Minor Compass Pt (dark)
(cut 4)

COMPASS
3–Major Compass Pt (dark)
(cut 4)

COMPASS
7–Background
(Cut 4)

▣ Just Plain Quilting

This technique requires no preliminary patchwork or appliqué assembly. Simply transfer the outline design to your fabric, add batting and backing layers to make a sandwich, and quilt the square using either quilting thread or embroidery floss in a matching or contrasting color.

Keep in mind that "just plain quilting" squares can be combined with appliqué and/or patchwork squares for larger projects such as the throw shown on page 17. Most of the large quilting designs (pages 99–108) will fill a 12-inch square. The smaller designs (pages 109–111) are good for smaller projects such as coasters and placemats or the trim on children's clothes. The small quilting designs also make good templates for overall quilting or border quilting on any of your lighthouse projects.

You might want to make several "just plain quilting" pillows, such as those shown on page 28, to accompany an appliqué lighthouse quilt.

Materials Needed

> fabric squares for top and backing (sized for your
> individual project)
> batting for individual project
> dressmaker's carbon or quilt marker (see note
> following step 4)
> masking tape
> embroidery floss or quilting thread

Preparing the Square

1. Place fabric square right side up on a hard surface. Tape the corners to the surface, making sure the fabric is held flat and taut.

2. Place dressmaker's carbon on the fabric, carbon side down. Tape it down too.

3. Place the quilting pattern on the carbon. Tape it in several places.

4. Starting in the upper left-hand corner, trace all the lines, ending back at the beginning. You will be less apt to miss tracing part of the pattern this way.

Note: If your fabric is light enough that the pattern lines can show through, you may not need to use the dressmaker's carbon. Instead, place pattern on a flat surface and the fabric square on top of it. Trace with a water-soluble quilt marker.

5. The marked square, now referred to as the top, is ready to be used in a project. If you have chosen to include the square in a larger project, set it aside until you have marked and assembled all the squares for the project.

For a single-square project, make a sandwich of top, batting, and backing. Baste. (Basting stitches are shown as dashed lines in the sketch below.)

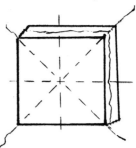

6. Using quilting thread or two strands of embroidery floss, quilt along all the traced lines. Press.

7. To complete your project, follow the directions in the "Projects, Projects, Projects" chapter.

This bell pattern lends itself well to both appliqué and "just plain quilting." It makes a wonderful Christmas design. Choose a check or plaid for a country theme; velvet, brocade, or gold for a more formal look. It could be used on placemats, a tablecloth, or pillows.

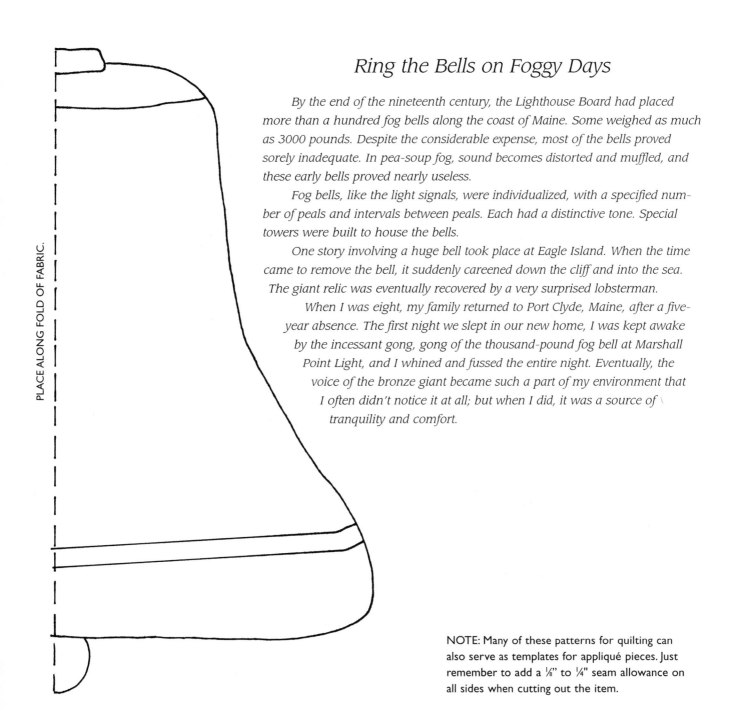

PLACE ALONG FOLD OF FABRIC.

Ring the Bells on Foggy Days

By the end of the nineteenth century, the Lighthouse Board had placed more than a hundred fog bells along the coast of Maine. Some weighed as much as 3000 pounds. Despite the considerable expense, most of the bells proved sorely inadequate. In pea-soup fog, sound becomes distorted and muffled, and these early bells proved nearly useless.

Fog bells, like the light signals, were individualized, with a specified number of peals and intervals between peals. Each had a distinctive tone. Special towers were built to house the bells.

One story involving a huge bell took place at Eagle Island. When the time came to remove the bell, it suddenly careened down the cliff and into the sea. The giant relic was eventually recovered by a very surprised lobsterman.

When I was eight, my family returned to Port Clyde, Maine, after a five-year absence. The first night we slept in our new home, I was kept awake by the incessant gong, gong of the thousand-pound fog bell at Marshall Point Light, and I whined and fussed the entire night. Eventually, the voice of the bronze giant became such a part of my environment that I often didn't notice it at all; but when I did, it was a source of tranquility and comfort.

NOTE: Many of these patterns for quilting can also serve as templates for appliqué pieces. Just remember to add a ⅛" to ¼" seam allowance on all sides when cutting out the item.

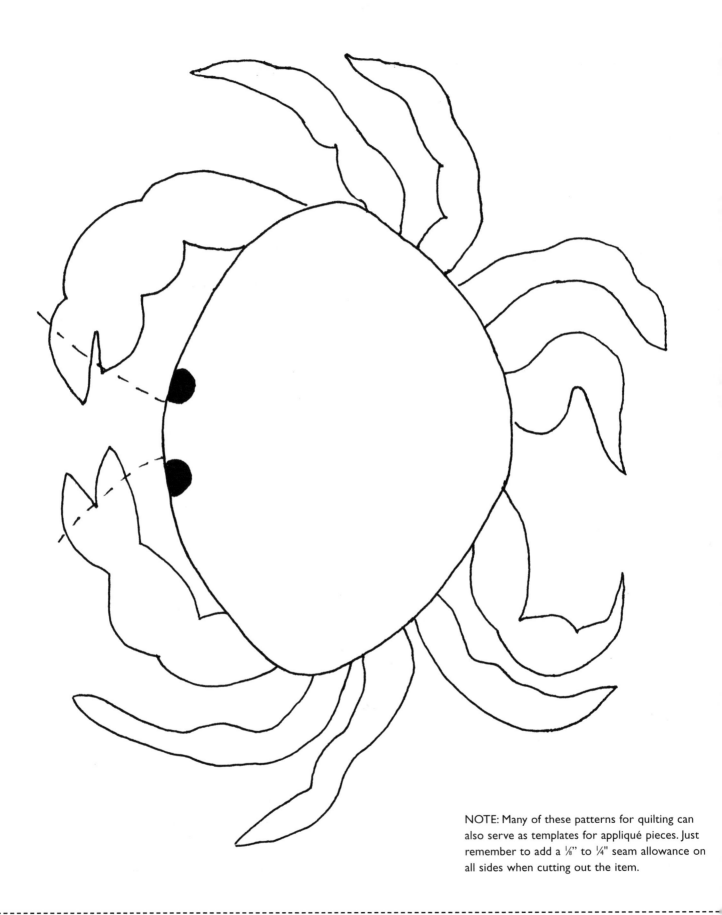

NOTE: Many of these patterns for quilting can also serve as templates for appliqué pieces. Just remember to add a ⅛" to ¼" seam allowance on all sides when cutting out the item.

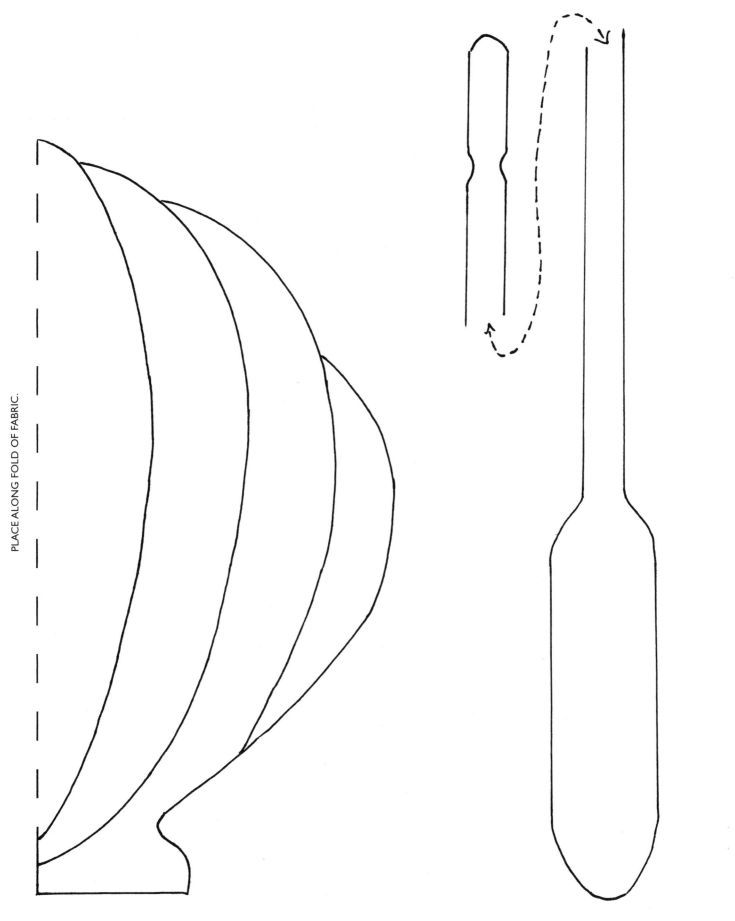

PLACE ALONG FOLD OF FABRIC.

NOTE: Many of these patterns for quilting can also serve as templates for appliqué pieces. Just remember to add a ⅛" to ¼" seam allowance on all sides when cutting out the item.

NOTE: To use these cloud patterns for appliqué pieces, add a ⅛" to ¼" seam allowance on all sides when cutting.

PLACE ALONG FOLD OF FABRIC.

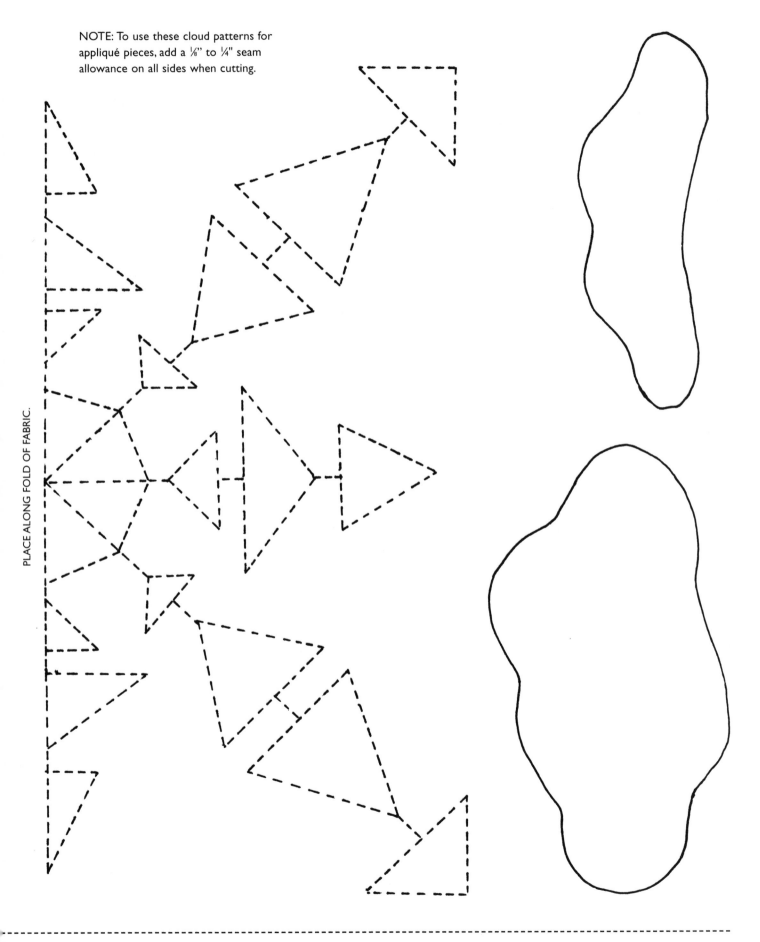

MATCH TO PATTERN ON P. 105.

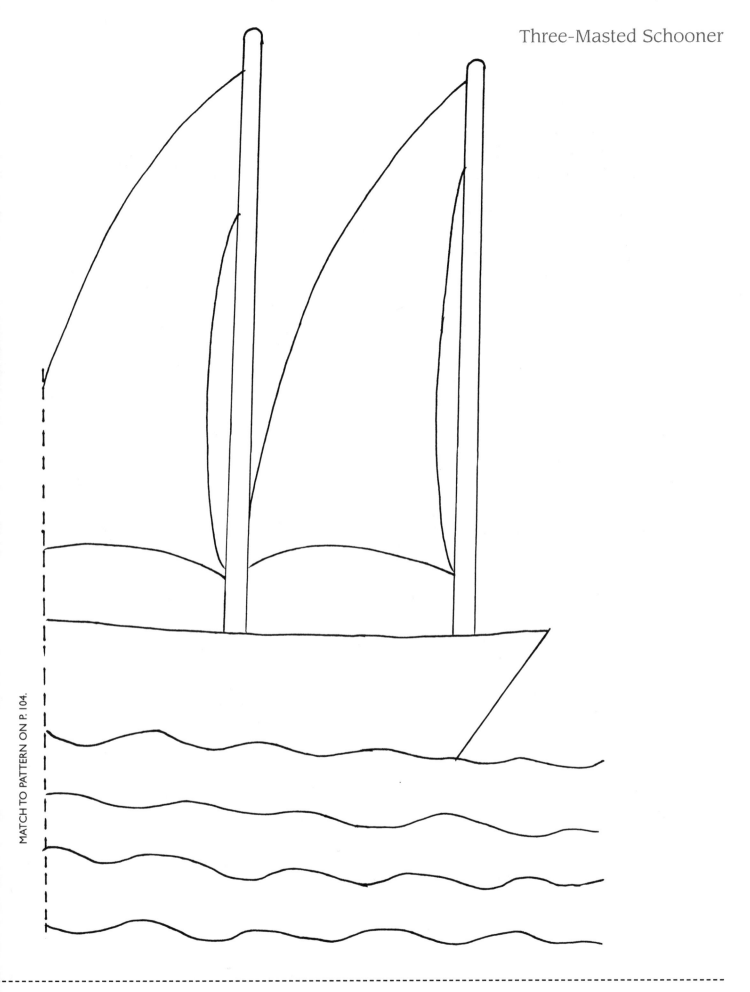

MATCH TO PATTERN ON P. 104.

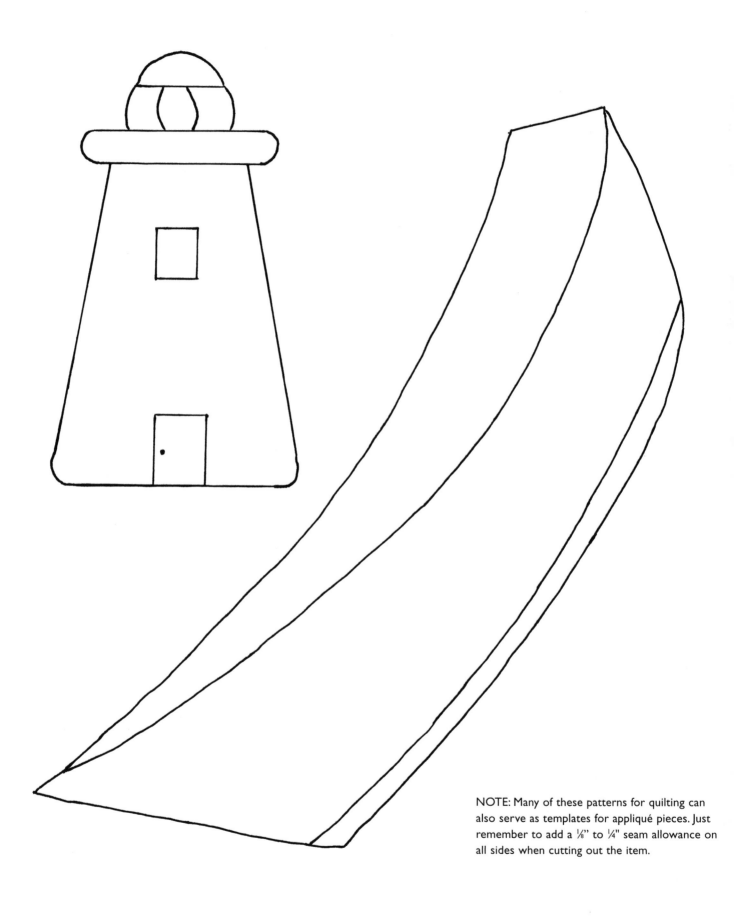

NOTE: Many of these patterns for quilting can also serve as templates for appliqué pieces. Just remember to add a ⅛" to ¼" seam allowance on all sides when cutting out the item.

NOTE: Many of these patterns for quilting can also serve as templates for appliqué pieces.
Just remember to add a ⅛" to ¼" seam allowance on all sides when cutting out the item.

NOTE: Many of these patterns for quilting can also serve as templates for appliqué pieces. Just remember to add a ⅛" to ¼" seam allowance on all sides when cutting out the item.

NOTE: Many of these patterns for quilting can also serve as templates for appliqué pieces. Just remember to add a ⅛" to ¼" seam allowance on all sides when cutting out the item.

NOTE: Many of these patterns for quilting can also serve as templates for appliqué pieces. Just remember to add a ⅛" to ¼" seam allowance on all sides when cutting out the item.

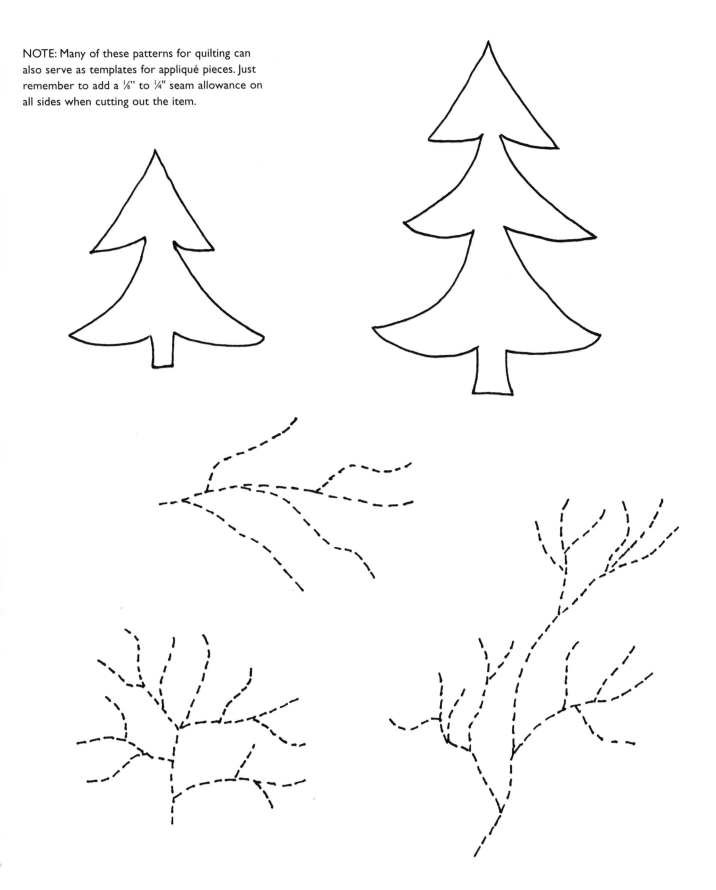

▣ To Learn More About Maine Lighthouses

Adamson, Hans Christian. *Keepers of the Lights.* New York, NY: Greenberg, 1955.

Caldwell, Bill. *Lighthouses of Maine.* Portland, ME: Gannett Books, 1986.

Clifford, J. Candace, and Mary Louise Clifford. *Nineteenth-Century Lights.* Alexandria, VA: Cypress Communications, 2000.

Coffin, Robert P. Tristram. *Kennebec: Cradle of Americans.* NY: Farrar and Rhinehart, 1937. Reprint edition Camden, ME: Down East Books, 2002.

Davidson, Donald W. *Lighthouses of New England: From the Maritimes to Montauk. Edison, NJ*: Wellfleet Press, 1990.

Duff, Elizabeth J. *Welcome to Castine: History of Castine.* The Castine Historical Society, n.d.

Simpson, Dorothy. *The Maine Islands in Story and Legend.* Philadelphia: J. B. Lippincott Company, 1960.

Sterling, Robert Thayer. *Lighthouses of the Maine Coast and the Men Who Keep Them.* Brattleboro, VT: Stephen Daye Press, 1935.

Stiles, Dan. *Land of Enchantment.* Concord, NH: Sugar Ball Press, 1945.

Swett, Sophie. *Stories of Maine.* New York: American Book Company, 1899.

Thompson, Courtney. *Maine Lighthouses: A Pictorial Guide.* Mount Desert, ME: CatNap Publications, 1996.

Witney Dudley. *The Lighthouse.* Boston: New York Graphic Society, 1975.